W9-DAP-231

Human
Mourning

EL

EMERGENT LITERATURES

An American Story
Jacques Godbout

In One Act
Adrienne Kennedy

Love in Two Languages
Abdelkebir Khatibi

Little Mountain
Elias Khoury

The Passion According to G. H.
Clarice Lispector

The Stream of Life
Clarice Lispector

The Trickster of Liberty
Gerald Vizenor

José
Revueltas

Human
Mourning

Introduction by Octavio Paz

University of Minnesota Press · Minneapolis

Copyright © 1990 by the Regents of the University of Minnesota

Original edition, *El luto humano*, copyright © 1980 by Ediciones Era, S.A. de C.V.; first published by Editorial Mexico in 1943.

Preface copyright © 1943, 1979 by Octavio Paz

All rights reserved. No part of this publication may be reproduced, stored in a retrieval system, or transmitted, in any form or by any means, electronic, mechanical, photo-copying, recording, or otherwise, without the prior written permission of the publisher.

Published by the University of Minnesota Press
2037 University Avenue Southeast, Minneapolis, MN 55414.

Printed in the United States of America
Cover and book design by Patricia M. Boman.

Library of Congress Cataloging-in-Publication Data

Revueltas, José, 1914–1976.
    [Luto humano. English]
    Human mourning / José Revueltas ; translation by Roberto Crespi.
      p.   cm. — (Emergent literatures)
    Translation of : El luto humano.
    ISBN 0-8166-1809-7. — ISBN 0-8166-1810-0 (pbk.)
    I. Title. II. Series.
PQ7297.R383L813   1989   89-35315
863—dc20   CIP

PQ
7297
.R383
L813
1989

FRANKLIN PIERCE
COLLEGE LIBRARY
RINDGE. N. H. 03461

The University of Minnesota is an equal-opportunity educator and employer.

"Because death is infinitely a loving act."

–Alberto Quintero Alvarez

Christianity and Revolution
Two Reviews of José Revueltas's *Human Mourning*
by Octavio Paz

First Review: 1943

When the armed struggle ended, and when what has come to be known as the "constructive stage of the Mexican Revolution" began, two different forms of artistic expression, the novel and painting, looked eagerly toward the immediate past. The results of this seduction have come to be known as the "school of Mexican painting" and the "novel of the Mexican Revolution." During the past twenty years, the novel has served to express more than the literary attempts of its authors, their revolutionary nostalgias, hopes, and disappointments. Technically flawed, these works are more picturesque than descriptive, more a literature of manners than realistic. The novelists of the Revolution, and among them the great miopic talent of Mariano Azuela, blinded by the fury of gunpowder or by that of the generals' diamonds, have reduced its theme to this: a lot of deaths, a lot of crimes, and lies; and a superficial scenario of burned villages, delirious jungles, or impious deserts. In this way they have mutilated the novelistic reality—the only one that counts for the true novelist—by reducing it to a pure chronicle or to a portrait of manners. All the "novels of the Revolution," not excluding those of Mariano Azuela, are stories and chronicles. (Valery Larbaud once said that Azuela reminded him of Tacitus: strange praise indeed for a novelist!)

The following generation has hardly even attempted the novel. Composed of a group of literary figures, poets, and essayists, it has shown a certain revulsion, if not contempt, for the realities that surround them. The novel has been the Cinderella of these writers who have been formed under the sign of curiosity and evasion. After them, there have indeed existed isolated attempts: those of the most recent group of writers, almost all of whom reveal a definite love for that difficult and strict genre of the short story. So, just as has happened in the case of the generation of the "muralists" in painting, a group of young writers, whom that benevolent Yankee criticism has called the "small masters," new Mexican prose writers, successors of the "novelists of the Revolution," have been distinguished, above all, in the composition of short stories and narrations.

The most ambitious and passionate—and also the youngest—is José Revueltas (27 years old: a member, since the age of fourteen, of the Mexican Communist Party; his political ideas, during the epoch of President Abelardo Rodríguez, have allowed him to know the country's prisons several times). José Revueltas has published his first novel, *El luto humano* (*Human Mourning*), winner of a national competition. Earlier he had written several mysterious and awkward stories, a short novel—*El quebranto* ("Affliction")—and a testimonial narration, *Los muros de agua* ("Walls of Water"), in which he tells the story of life in a Pacific penal colony. (He was imprisoned there for two years, while still in his teens, accused of conspiracy.) Revueltas's novel has managed to ignite, at the same time, the most exalted praise and the most bitter criticism. One Marxist critic has accused Revueltas of "pessimism"; on the other hand, others, more en-

thusiastic, have not hesitated to compare him with Dostoevsky.

Human Mourning narrates a dramatic story: a group of
peasants declare a strike in one of the "Irrigation Systems"
sponsored by the Revolution. The strike and the lack of water
cause the government project to fail, and the exodus begins.
Only three families stubbornly decide to remain on the
parched land. One day, the river, dry up until then, begins to
rise excessively, and a flood isolates the novel's protagonists
on a rooftop. Alcohol, hunger, and jealousies finish them off.
The novel begins when the river is rising, and it ends at the
moment the buzzards make ready to devour the dead. All this
takes place within a few days. But the novel only barely al-
ludes to what the peasants actually do to escape the flood;
Revueltas prefers to tell us what they think, what they remember, and what they feel. He frequently substitutes for his protagonists; he erases them and, in their place, he gives us his
own doubts, his own faith and desperation, his own opinions
about death or about Mexican religiosity. The action is interrupted each time one of the protagonists, before dying, reviews his life (on occasion true events, extraneous to the novel
and very artificially placed within it). A constant religious
preoccupation invades the work: Mexicans, devout by nature
and lovers of blood, have been stripped of their religion, Catholicism unable to satisfy their stonelike and bloody thirst
for eternity. Adán, an assassin who believes himself to be the
incarnation of Fate, and Natividad, an assassinated leader,
symbolize, very religiously, the past and future of Mexico. Between them move the present-day, rancorous Mexicans; their
voiceless women represent the earth, thirsty for water and
blood, a baptism that combines, together with the rites of agricultural fertility, the ancient baptism of the Aztecs and that
of the Christians. In the final pages, the author attempts to
convince himself — more than the reader — that through a bet-

ter distribution of wealth, this religiosity without hope, this blind love of death, will disappear from the soul of Mexico. The novel, as can be seen, is contaminated with sociology, religion, and the ancient and present history of Mexico. The same can be said of its language, at times brilliant, at times strangely awkward.

These defects condemn the work, but not its author. Because, strangely, the reader feels infected by the fascination of which the novelist is victim. Revueltas feels a kind of religious disgust, a love of horror and revulsion, toward Mexico. Surely Revueltas has not written a novel; instead, he has shed some light within himself. Seduced by the myths of Mexico as much as by its realities, he has made himself part of that drama that he is attempting to paint. Blessed with unusual talent, imaginative force, vigor, and sensitivity—and devoured by a haste that apparently did not permit him to correct his defects—José Revueltas can now write a novel. In any case, in this attempt he has freed himself from all his ghosts, all his doubts and all his opinions. As has occurred with a large part of Mexican painting, which shows a great vigor that many times remains outside the painting, outside the canvas, Revueltas has accumulated, without rhyme or reason, all the great plastic and divinatory power of this vigor, but without succeeding in applying it to his object: the novel. What is it, in conclusion, that I reproach in Revueltas? I reproach him—and now I realize it—his youth; because in all these defects, this lack of sobriety in his language, this desire to say everything all at once, this dispersion and this laziness to cut the useless wings of words, ideas, and situations, this absence of discipline—interior and exterior—are nothing more than defects of youth. In any case, Revueltas is the first among us to attempt to create a profound work, far from the ruling novel of manners, superficiality, and cheap psychology. Perhaps there will remain only the slightest breath from his work: but is this not sufficient for a young writer who is only now beginning, and initiating us in the process, the mission of creating for us an imaginative and strangely and disturbingly personal world?

Mexico, 1943

Second Review: 1979

When I reread the review printed above, published in an old issue of the journal *Sur*, I immediately felt the need to clarify and extend it. It is the criticism of one beginner of another; moreover, it is too cutting and categorical. My excuse is that these defects are frequent in young writers. In the end, I reproach Revueltas for his youth and that very same criticism is perfectly applicable to my opinions at that time. Youth does not, however, justify other errors. For example, in the first paragraph I condemn the novelists of the Mexican Revolution. It was a foolish mistake: among them are two excellent writers, Martín Luis Guzmán and Mariano Azuela. Both were masters of their art. Martín Luis Guzmán's prose, as sharp as that of a Roman historian, possesses a kind of classical transparency: his subject is dreadful, but he portrays it with a calm and steady hand. Azuela was not "a great miopic talent"; nor was he incompetent: he was a lucid writer, in control of his resources, who explored many roads others have since traveled. But when I wrote my review of *Human Mourning* (1943), the novel of the Revolution had already been transformed into a school: invention had already become formula. In this sense, I was not mistaken: the appearance of *Human Mourning*, published a few years before Agustín Yáñez's *Al filo del agua* (1947) (*On the Edge of the Storm*), was a rupture and a beginning. With this novel, and in spite of its imperfections, Revueltas began something that has not yet come to an end.

My analysis of *Human Mourning* is too brisk. I point out with excessive severity the narrator's inexperience and the frequency with which his voice substitutes for those of his characters. These defects are due, at least in part, to the difficulty and newness of what Revueltas was attempting to say and what, years later, he was able to say with greater success. The young novelist wanted to use the new techniques of the North American novel (the presence of the Faulkner of *Wild Palm Trees* is constant) to write a chronicle, both epic and symbolic, of an episode that seemed to him endowed with a revolutionary exemplariness. The objective was contradictory: Faulkner's realism (like all realism, perhaps) implies a pessimistic vision of man and his earthly fate; whereas Revueltas's epic chronicle is mined, so to speak, with religious symbolism. The peasants struggle for land and water, but the novelist continually suggests that this struggle refers to another struggle that is not entirely of this world. Although my 1943 review emphasizes Revueltas's religiosity, it does not describe its paradoxical character: a vision of Christianity within his Marxist atheism. Revueltas lived Marxism as Christianity, and that is why he lived it, as Unamuno would put it, as agony, doubt, and negation.

When I speak about the religiosity of the Mexican people, I use the term "rancorous," an imprecise word. I attribute it to the great catastrophe of the Conquest, which not only shattered the Indians' world but also that other world of their gods and mythologies. Nevertheless, in opening up the doors of heaven and hell with the key of baptism, Catholicism paradoxically granted the Indians the possibility of reconciliation with their ancient religion. Perhaps Revueltas thought that "on a higher historical plain," revolutionary Marxism, as opposed to Christianity, would carry out the same function Christianity had with respect to the pre-Columbian religions. This idea would explain the importance of the Christian symbolism in the novel. Moreover, he was always fascinated by popular beliefs and myths. A friend has told me that Revueltas, once, half in jest and half in earnest, thought of celebrating his marriage vows not in front of the Virgin of Guadalupe but rather in front of the goddess Coatlicue in the Museum of Anthropology. I remember also that the night of the Corpus Christi massacre of 1971, several friends had assembled in Carlos Fuentes's home, and, while we discussed what to do, Revueltas came up to me and, with an indefinable smile, whispered in my ear: "Let's all go and dance in front of Santo Señor de Chalma!" A phrase can reveal a man: "atheism," André Breton once told me, "is an act of faith." Revueltas's wit and ideas were oblique confessions.

At the end of my review, I note the real significance of *Human Mourning*: "Revueltas has not written a novel but instead he has shed some light within himself." Today I would say: that work was one step in his pilgrimage, a true calvary, toward that light. And here we have the central question, the one which Revueltas bravely faced with his very first story, *El quebranto* ("Affliction"), and which he never ceased asking: what light, this one or the one over there? Perhaps here is there, perhaps revolutions are nothing but the road that runs from here to there. Revueltas's activities seem secretly inspired by this idea. He was a revolutionary militant, a novelist, and the author of philosophical and political essays. As a militant, he was a dissident who criticized capitalism and bureaucratic "socialism" with identical passion; this same duality can be observed in his novels, stories, and essays. So, on the one hand, there is a great unity between his life and his work: it is impossible to separate the novelist from the militant and the militant from the author of texts of philosophical, aesthetic, and political criticism; on the other hand, this unity contains a fracture, a split. Revueltas was in constant dialogue—or, more exactly, in permanent dispute—with his philosophical, aesthetic, and political ideas. His criticism of orthodox communism was simultaneously self-criticism. His case, of course, is not unique; on the contrary, it is more and more common: the dissidence of Marxist intellectuals is one of the expressions, perhaps the central expression, of the universal crisis of that doctrine. But there is something that does distinguish Revueltas's doubts and criticisms from the others: tone and religious passion. And there's something else: the questions Revueltas asks himself over and over make no sense and cannot be elucidated except within a religious perspective. Not that of any religion, but precisely that of Christianity.

For Westerners, the opposition between atheism and religion is insurmountable. This has not been the case for other civilizations: in its strictest and purest form, Buddhism is atheistic. Nevertheless, that atheism does not eradicate the divine: like all living beings, men and the Buddha himself included, gods are bubbles, reflections of vacuity. Buddhism is a radical critique of reality and the human condition: the true reality, *sunyata*, is an indefinable state in which being and non-being, the real and the unreal, cease to be opposites and, upon fusing, are mutually canceled. Therefore, history is nothing but phantasmagoria, illusion—like everything else. Buddhist religiosity, therefore, is also essentially contemplative. On the other hand, for Christianity, Jesus' incarnation and sacrifice are facts that are both supernatural and historical. Divine revelation not only displays itself in history, but it also is the testing ground for Christians: souls are won and lost here, in this world. The Marxist Revueltas assumes, with all its consequences, the Christian legacy: the weight of men's history.

The connection between Christianity and Marxism is history; they are both doctrines identified with the historical process. The condition of possibility for Marxism is the same as that for Christianity: action in this world. At the same time, the opposition between Marxism and Christianity is revealed here on earth: to fulfill himself and his mission, revolutionary man has to evict God from history. The first revolutionary act is the critique of heaven. The relationship between Marxism and Christianity implies, simultaneously, a bond and a rupture. Buddhism—in general, all Eastern thought—ignores or is contemptuous of history. At the same time, immersed in the atmosphere of the divine, surrounded by gods, it is unfamiliar with the notion of only one God, the creator. Eastern atheism is not truly atheism; in a strict sense, only Jews, Christians, and Muslims can be atheists: believers in one God, the creator. Bloch has very correctly said: "Only a true Christian can be a good atheist; only a true atheist can be a good Christian."

Revueltas's Christian Marxism is intelligible only from the double perspective I have just outlined. In the first place, the idea of history conceived as a process endowed with meaning and direction; in the second place, irreducible atheism. Between history and atheism a new opposition opens up: if God disappears, history loses its meaning. Christian atheism is tragic because, as Nietzsche has seen, it is the negation of meaning. For Dostoevsky, if there is no God, everything is permitted, everything is possible; but if everything is possible, nothing is possible; the infinity of possibilities cancels all possibilities and is resolved in impossibility. In the same way, the absence of God makes everything thinkable; but everything is equal to nothing; everything and nothing are not thinkable; that is why it is terrifying and, literally, intolerable. Also, that is why we have installed in God's vacancy other divinities: Reason, Progress. These principles come down to earth, are incarnated, and become the secret actors of history. They are our Christs; the nation, the proletariat, the race. In Revueltas's novel, ancient man is called Adán (Adam) like our father; and the new man, the collective Christ, is called Natividad (Christmas). The story of the Son of Man begins with Birth and culminates in Sacrifice; the Revolution obeys the same logic. That logic is rational, "scientific": historical materialism; and it is supernatural: transcendence. The "scientific" is explicit; the supernatural, implicit. Divine transcendence disappears, but, surreptitiously, it continues to operate. But, as Bloch himself has said, the revolution is "transcending without transcendence."

The enmity between Marxism and Christianity never totally disappears, but it is mitigated if the terms change positions. For Christianity men are the sons of Adam, the son of God. In the beginning, there is God, who is not only the giver of meaning, but the creator of life. God is before history and at the conclusion of it: He is the beginning and the end. For a Christian Marxist like Bloch or Revueltas, God cannot be before; actually, God does not exist; the original and primordial reality is man, or rather, human society. But historical man is barely a man; to realize himself, to be truly a man, man must pass through the tests of history, he must overcome and transform his fatality into freedom. Revolution makes men of men — and more than men: the future of man is to be God. Christianity was the humanization of a God; Revolution promises the deification of men. An abrupt changing of positions: God is not before but after, not the creator of men, but their creation. Block changes the Biblical phrase and says: *I am he who will be (L'Athéisme dans le Christianisme)*.

Revueltas never formulated his ideas with Bloch's clarity, but the mood of his writings and his life corresponds to this moribund and contradictory vision of Marxism and Christianity. Of course, he arrived at these attitudes independently and traveling his own road. It was not philosophy that guided him, but rather his personal experience. In the first place, the life of the Mexican people, totally impregnated with religiosity; and, finally, his own philosophical and poetic temperament. This last factor was decisive: Revueltas asked himself philosophical questions that Marxism — as Kolakowski and Bloch himself, among others, have recognized — cannot answer except by scientific clichés. In reality, those questions only have metaphysical or religious answers. Metaphysics, after Hume and Kant, has been prohibited to us modern men. So, Revueltas, intuitively and passionately, in a movement of return to the oldest part of his being, consulted religious answers mixed with the millenary ideas and hopes of the revolutionary movement. Although philosophy excited him, he was above all a creative artist. His religious temperament led him to communism, which he saw as the road of sacrifice and communion; that same temperament, inseparable from the love of truth and goodness, led him at the end of his life to the criticism of bureaucratic "socialism" and Marxist clericalism.

Marxism has been converted into an ideology, and today it operates as a pseudo-religion. The transformation of a philosophy into an ideology and then into a religion is not a new phenomenon; the same thing happened with neo-Platonism and gnosticism. Nor is the transformation of a religion into political power new, nor that of the priesthood into clerical bureaucracy: Catholicism is well familiar with these perversions. The historical peculiarity of communism is the fact that it is really not a religion, but rather an ideology that operates as if it were a science, the Science; at the same time, it is not a church, but a party that does not resemble the other parties but rather the militant orders and brotherhoods of Catholics and Muslims. Communist parties always begin as small sects, but as soon as they begin to grow they become closed churches. (I am using the plural because in the communist movement splits and schisms proliferate.) Each church believes itself to be the possessor of universal truth; this pretension would not be dangerous if the bureaucracies that run these groups were not moved by an equally universal will of domination and proselytism. Each member of each church is a missionary, and each missionary is a potential inquisitor. Revueltas's religiosity was far removed from those ideological fanaticisms; his true spiritual affinities are to be found elsewhere, near the primitive Christians, the gnostics of the fourth century, or the rebellious and revolutionary Protestants of the Reformation. Within the Catholic Church, he would have been a heretic, as indeed he was within orthodox communism. His Marxism was not a system but rather a passion, not a faith but rather a doubting, and, to use Bloch's word, a hope.

Living with himself was not, for Revueltas, less difficult than living with his communist comrades. For many years he tried to be a disciplined militant, and each attempt resulted in rupture and expulsion. Hegelian dialectics were useful to him in postponing the definitive rupture; like so many others, he told himself that evil is a trick of history so as to better fulfill itself, that negation is a moment of the process that inevitably is transformed into affirmation, that revolutionary tyrants are tyrants in order to defend freedom, and that—as the Spanish theologians in the seventeenth century and the Procurator Vishinski and the Bolsheviks prosecuted in 1936 and 1938 have confirmed brilliantly in the twentieth—the guilty are innocent and the innocent guilty. Enigmas of divine will or of historical necessity. The justification of evil began with Plato; in his retractions and abjurations, Revueltas did nothing more than follow a tradition of more than two thousand years. According to the neo-Platonist Proclus, matter itself "is good, in spite of being infinite, obscure and formless." (For the ancients, infinity was an imperfection because it lacked form.) But the resources of the dialectic are used up as evil grows without limits. Finally, Revueltas had to confront the reality of Bolshevism and his own reality. He did not resolve this conflict—who has?—but he had the courage to formulate and think it. He lived his internal contradiction with loyalty: his atheistic Christianity, his moribund Marxism. Many have praised the integrity with which he suffered imprisonment and poverty because of his ideas. It is true, but we must remember, in addition, that Revueltas practiced another no less difficult or austere heroism: intellectual heroism.

His work is uneven. Some of his pages seem, more than finished texts, to be rough drafts; others are noteworthy and have bestowed upon him a separate and unique place in Mexican literature: *Los días terrenales* ('Days on Earth'), *Los errores* ("The Errors"), *El apando* ("The Lock-up"), and, especially, the stories of *Dios en la tierra* ("God on Earth") and *Dormir en tierra* ("Sleeping on Shore"), many of them admirable. But the literary excellence of these works, which is truly considerable, does not explain fully the attraction that his figure commands. In our world, everything is relative, good and evil, pleasure and pain. Although most people are content, some rebel and, possessed by a god or a demon, demand everything. They thirst and hunger for the absolute. Don't ask me to define this: the absolute is by definition indefinable. Revueltas suffered that hunger and that thirst; to satisfy them he was a writer and a revolutionary. If I look among modern Mexicans for a kindred spirit, I have to go to the opposite ideological camp and to an earlier generation: José Vasconcelos. Like Revueltas, he had a passionate temperament, but he was unable to subject his passion to discipline, a writer of impulses and guesses, prolific and careless, sometimes awkward and other times brilliant. For both, political action and metaphysical adventure, historical polemics, and meditation were communicating vessels. They united active life with contemplative or, rather, speculative life: in their works, there is really no disinterested contemplation—for me, the supreme wisdom—but rather meditation, reflection, and, in their best moments, spiritual flight. Vasconcelos's work is vaster and richer than Revueltas's, but not deeper nor more intense. But what I would like to underscore is that they belong to the same psychic family. They are contrasted to Alfonso Reyes, who made an absolute out of harmony, and to José Gorostiza, who adored perfection with such an exclusive love that he preferred to remain silent than to write something unworthy of it.

Despite their spiritual bond, Vasconcelos and Revueltas traveled opposite roads. Nourished on Plotinus and a believer in his mission of crowned philosopher, Vasconcelos felt sent from on high: that is why he was an educator; Revueltas believed in the rebel apostles, and he saw himself as sent from the world below: that is why he was a revolutionary. The spiritualist Vasconcelos never doubted: the world (power) and the flesh (women) tempted him. Vasconcelos confessed that he had coveted his neighbor's wife and that he had fornicated with her, but he never accepted that he had erred. The only sins the materialist Revueltas confessed were those of the spirit: doubts, denials, errors, white lies. In the end, he repented and criticized his ideas and the dogmas in which he had believed. Vasconcelos did not repent; he extolled Christian humility only to better smear his enemies with invectives; Revueltas, in the name of Marxist philosophy, undertook an examination of conscience that Saint Augustine and Pascal would have appreciated, and that impresses me for two reasons: for the scrupulous honor with which he carried it out, and for the subtlety and profundity of his analysis. Vasconcelos ended his life embracing Catholic clericalism; Revueltas broke with Marxist clericalism. Which of the two was the true Christian?

Mexico, 1979

Human
Mourning

I

Death was right there, white, sitting in the chair, with its face. The air, thick with feverish bells, penetrating injections, arsenic and burned alcohol, moved like the flame of a candle to the rhythm of the beating of those so very precious and cherished last breaths, breaths you could hear. You could hear them move from one side of the room to the other, from corner to corner, from the mosquito netting to the sheets, from the now opaque oil lamp to the graying window pane, like a pendulum. Death was right there, sitting in the chair.

"*Dios mío*, it's true! She's going to die!"

Within a few minutes death would leave the chair, penetrate the mosquito netting and disappear into that tiny body between the sheets. How else could one explain those breaths? How else could one explain that beating? And the flame, the air moving like a flame, slowly, slowly, from one side of the room to the other, from the oil lamp to the window, from the corner to the wall, swinging its dreadful, menacing mass back and forth. Such a small body with breathing so heavy that death could enter.

His wife, beside the small bed, turned toward him with an expression of piercing lucidity born of sorrow.

The scene became unbearable and he was already brac-

3

ing himself for the stupor all this would cause him, the terrifying numbness that would later spread throughout his mind. He therefore could not help but look once again to see if it was still right there, in the chair. But it had disappeared. Perhaps it had never been sitting there, with its white face; perhaps it had all been a kind of vision. But what was indeed certain was that, vision or not, it had disappeared.

His wife uttered something resembling a sound. Something that could not be explained with her voice (she probably said: "She's dead"), and then he could finally dare to move from where he had been standing to the side of the bed, where he tried to close the hard, tiny snap-shut eyes with his fingers. "Like a doll's eyes," he said to himself, "only stranger."

He began to feel stupefied, just as he had originally thought he would, and the consciousness of this stupor was the only intelligence that still moved in his dulled, dimmed mind.

Sinisterly active, his wife tenderly wrapped the tiny dead body in a shroud, but she did so with a kind of tragic boldness, as if she did not possess the emotional restraint necessary when in the presence of a corpse. She turned to look at her husband with determined, savage eyes:

"You can't refuse now!"

He could not in fact refuse now. He did not even bother to shake his head as he had done before, stubbornly and full of doubt; he felt stupefied by a great sadness. Death was no longer in the chair but neither, oh God, was it in that dead body. Because death is not dying but rather what precedes dying, what immediately precedes dying, when it has not yet entered the body and sits motionless and white, black, violet, and red, in the nearest chair.

"Yes," he said, since now it no longer mattered to him whether he went for the priest or not. "I'll go and get him."

Always a priest at the hour of death. A priest who cuts out the heart from the chest with that stone knife of penitence, to offer it, as did the ancient priests on the sacrificial stone, to God, to God in whose bosom the idols had been pulverized and their earth scattered, imperceptible now in the white body of divinity.

"I'm going," he insisted. "How could I not go?"

But his words revealed a deep resentment that he recognized as existing beyond everything.

He decided to wear his poncho because of the north wind and storm raging outside, so he headed for the hook that served as a clothes rack.

Then he thought about how she and he had furiously struggled with each other while the young child was dying. Initially he had refused to go for the priest. And he had refused despite the fact that it could have signified something terrible and momentous, desolate and hopeless. But maybe it was not a lie. Maybe it was the concrete and infinite truth of his wife's savage eyes imploring him to leave in search of the priest. She was imploring him with such a furious and stubborn terror and with such a look of condemnation in her eyes that the ritual, that is to say, the *sacrament* of confession, ceased being false and became mystery and truth: the restoration of the soul via a living and earthly man such as a priest, who does nothing but receive in his human ears the definitive, overwhelming narration of sin. "What about her?" he managed to think. "Why didn't she go herself?" But he immediately realized that she was incapable of moving, that she could not move as long as death was so close to the small bed, sitting right there in the chair. Because then everything would have happened earlier, during the desperate period in which the woman, crazed in the middle of the night, would have begun her search. No. The only one who could bring the sacraments, the sacramental objects, the red Catholic mysteries, the sacred oil, the burning stole, was he, he who remained frozen in place looking with insane grief at the green, blue death sitting in the chair.

Today everything seemed pointless, and if he were mistaken, if that purgatory of shadows, that sobbing and aimless wandering under the eyes of God of whom the Church spoke with such strong and choleric faith, really existed, then his daughter would suffer, and she would suffer even more than all she had already suffered on earth.

"If there's no other way, I'll swim across the river. I'll come back with the priest by dawn in any case."

His wife had hated him for an instant, when the child was still hopelessly gasping, but with a hatred so intense, vast, and heartless that that instant acquired the value of a lifetime, as if she had hated him for a thousand years.

He was going for the priest with rage. Neither eternal life nor eternal death, eternal and without limits, could exist. Nevertheless, that eternal life did in fact exist in his wife's eyes. Rage at going for the priest and at the fact that death perhaps knew no boundaries and was as infinite as a muscle of God. "In any case, he won't be able to save her soul now," he said to himself with sorrow, thinking of the dead child. And he turned to look at his wife, who with hardened jaws like clenched bones appeared to believe in God. "She is God, and she is the sacrament. God exists as much in her as He does not exist in me." But the truth was that it was not God but rather something else savagely and mercilessly demanding that that small death, that fugitive breath, be prepared and sacredly made ready for the mystery.

Before leaving he sat for a moment on the same chair on which death had been sitting to continue observing his wife, who had lit some candles. Where did those candles come from? It was as if she had had them ready for a long time. Outside, the north wind was raging.

After shrouding the body, the woman sat down on a small bench and she inexplicably appeared to be on her knees, begging for forgiveness, while she stared at the glowing, red forehead of the corpse, glowing from a light within. Merciful God, was she dead?

"I'll swim across if there's no other way," he insisted, with utter sorrow.

The north wind was pounding against the night. And the sky was void of light, extinguished, with thickly moving, enormous black masses, clouds or gigantic stones, or clouds of stone.

His wife, like a hope chest of grief, no longer said anything with her suddenly empty and glaring eyes; only an absurd solitude wrapped her with its damp veil. She had to busy herself with informing the neighbors so that they would come to stand vigil at the wake and drink, with their yellow and white flowers, if there were any to be found, so that they would come to say: "You know, Cecilia, how sorry we are. Ursulo, please accept our sympathy for the little angel." Little angel, little girl angel. And God was pounding the sky, that terrifying dark and starless celestial vault.

Cecilia turned her maternal face (so maternal that all of a sudden he, Ursulo, was just like her own child, like her own daughter, with his dark stare and his strange mortal eyes):

"Be careful with the river. It frightens me."

And then:

"If you can, bring some paraffin. And a little mescal or, if not, some alcohol."

Ursulo then departed into the night, putting on his poncho and experiencing the sensation of having penetrated the huge dark eye of a terrifying blind man. The sand was whirling about, getting into his roughly cut sandals and smashing against the straps, almost bursting them. It was a thick sand, as if the wind had become solid and its strange ingredients, its living oxygen, had also died, dispersing into multiple and infinite stone. "If only a priest lived here!" he lamented, because it was necessary to cross the river—cross it, make a cross—to reach the village where the church was. Sand and water, thrashing furiously in the night.

He walked confused and dazed for about half an hour, fighting with the air and the downpour. "Poor little Chonita has died," he said to himself, Chonita, his daughter's name. He said it to himself as if he were not her father. Nevertheless she was something much more precious, perhaps more cherished, than a daughter. An unexpected idea surged in his head in the middle of the night: the last sacrament, the final communication of sins, the last oil, the holy oils of the King of the Jews, was nothing other than immortality itself. Because death only exists without God, when God does not see us die. But when a priest arrives, God sees us die and He forgives us. He forgives us our life, the life He is about to snatch from us. These words, like hot embers, had already been said by Cecilia's eyes, when death was right there, white, and a breathing was invading the room, moving its walls and all walls. "It's true, she's dead," he had repeated, without for an instant taking his eyes off his daughter's body and totally stunned by the brutal conviction of his thoughts.

He walked aimlessly, without direction and with great abandon, trusting in who knows what to reach the river.

When a storm brings light with it and its fury becomes more visible and its momentum less blind, the human heart is not startled by emptiness or infinite notions. It senses a distant stab of hope. But when in the night the wind is unleashed and its thousand chains thrash the earth, the human spirit returns to its origins, to its beginnings, when all that existed was the tremendous anticipation of moaning.

He stumbled over a fence in the middle of the crushing darkness. What? Where was he? The indifferent and chaotic wind of water surrounding him was wailing. Then Ursulo felt that, because of his deep sorrow and the numerous ideas pounding in his head, he had strayed off course.

He banged on the fence:

"Am I far from the river?"

And was he really very far, independently of whether or not someone answered his cries and oriented him?

Inside a small noise was heard and then the predictable, suspicious and muffled voice:

"What do you want?"

'The river . . . to cross it."

The river, serpent of black and aggressive water, muddied by the storm, its bed hurled up to the agitated surface.

As if in a dream, the nocturnal distrust, which constantly expected an enemy in the shadows, also caused a woman's voice to speak, whispering beside her husband:

"Your machete."

The metal clanged inside.

"You're going to the river at this time of night and in this storm?"

Ursulo felt the terrible anguish that perhaps they would not open the door.

"I'm going for the priest."

"He's lying," thought the other man. "It's Ursulo who's come to ambush me."

"Come right out and tell me what you want, Ursulo."

Ursulo said nothing. He was now beginning to think that they were going to kill him. That they would open the door and attack him with a machete. That this man never forgave. He was now in God's hands.

"Cecilia has lost the child; she's dead."

Cecilia, as if the child were not also his, although it was Cecilia indeed who had lost her.

Then he heard how the machete was smoothly, even gently, placed back on the hook. And the resentful, although also somewhat moved, voice:

"Come in!"

Perhaps they hated each other. Now together, the one facing the other, there were no words; there was only an undefined staring of impenetrable blind eyes.

"You've come to ambush me, so go ahead," he told Ursulo without moving from where he stood, as if he were far away, as if he had uttered other words.

Ursulo shook his head, sadly denying the accusation:

"I got lost with this north wind. I have no weapon. Chonita really died."

He explained that he was going for the priest, that he wanted to cross the river.

And they remained silent, in muted combat.

Inside, everything was made of earth; there was no furniture, just a chair and an old grinding stone as dark as an iguana. Cuts of dried beef hung from the ceiling, well-smoked, with its human, Indian and copper color.

"The child has gone, the little angel has flown away," Adán thought, because all children are small angels who fly. And he looked at Ursulo's sad, exhausted shoulders, and his lowered head and his eyes thick with bitter tenderness.

"You have my sympathy," he mumbled.

The wind had a way of pounding against the sand and the water. An obstinate and somber way. In an obstinate and somber country.

The only reason they could no longer kill each other, as they stood there face to face, was because they were separated by a death physically alien to them both.

"So let's go!" said Adán.

Ursulo raised his eyes, but he could not make out anything in Adán's eyes because there was nothing in them but the distant *tezontle*, the volcanic rock of a race as ancient as the wind. "Adán, son of God. The first man."

"Let's go!"

The woman's suspicious she-wolf glare, she-wolf body, and she-wolf breath attempted a warning, a gesture:

"Your machete, Adán."

Adán looked at her and who knows what his eyes of stone said as they cut into the woman like a knife.

They left. Adán, without his machete, naked, without the fig leaf.

He had a small boat for buying *aguardiente*, matches, oil, dried beef, cloth, needles, and mirrors in the village on the other side of the river. With a burning iron he had branded the letters *La Cautibadora** on one side of the boat, the letters deep-set around the labial letter b.

Their sense of smell led them to the river, but there was also another sense, a kind of convergence of all the senses, as if the river's running tongue were perceived without being seen by the eyes, without being heard by the ears, without being touched, precisely because man is also water that runs and flows, collecting mud and impurities in its course, some of which are defiled and others immaculate.

"I got lost in the north wind, in the darkness," said Ursulo, "and I wound up at your house."

The Indians had given Adán the boat to keep him happy when he was Municipal Agent in the Sierra. Adán possessed that poisoned *sangre mestiza*, or mixed blood, in which the Indians saw their own fear and discovered their own eternal nostalgia, their retrospective terror, the total shipwreck they could not forget.

"I thought you were coming to kill me," he answered.

"No. I didn't come to kill you."

*Misspelling of *La Cautivadora* ("The Captivating One")

They were silent for a moment, and then Adán:

"I was a little afraid."

One of these two men was one too many in this world. Who he would be was to be decided by metal, silent ambush, and shadows.

The destructive and menacingly close river was thundering, so black that it could have been in the air, a celestial river, in that darkness of heaven and earth where feet became the only things sure and essential.

La Cautibadora, close by, was already speaking its language of pounded wood. They climbed in.

Below their knees they felt the coldness of the water that was filling *La Cautibadora*, and they began to bail the water out by hand, producing a sound like that of a palatal click.

"Will he throw me into the river?" thought Ursulo, and once again he thought about penetrating the meaning of that mask, of that enigmatic density that was Adán's. "Not now, not now that Chonita has died," he answered himself. And something so illogical, so extraordinary and so strange as this thought could only have occurred to him because so too was the land of this country: tender, cruel, hostile, torrid, frigid, friendly, indifferent, evil, bitter, pure.

He thought about everything Adán owed (Adán, father of Cain, father of Abel): about the lives he *owed*, those of which he was the *debtor*, as they put it, because killing is a *debt*; about the sturdy, harsh Cain of which he was made; about the dead and buried names of Natividad, Valentín, Guadalupe, Gabriel, whom Adán had erased from the earth. "The people say that he owes more than five deaths." And who knows why they say "*more* than five" when it was possible that he had killed only five. But they had been a humiliated people for many years and many centuries, humiliated from birth; and the word *more* simply indicated that the criminal—or the usual criminals—would continue to kill.

"*More* than five." *More. More.* Pure fatalism, sad and ancient resignation, where an internal, obedient apathy, inevitable and disconsolate, awaited new crimes and more and more dead victims without resisting.

They had untied the boat and were heading toward the deep water.

Why was it that the oars could be heard so clearly in the middle of the storm? Even though they were quite long they were insignificant and small against the river and the un-leashed sky. Their sound ought not to have been heard when the storm's wailing was everywhere. It was as if the river were made of earth and the oars were shovels moving over the emptiness of another land, a funereal and forsaken land. A river of earth. Tomorrow Chonita would be under the earth.

"We're alone," said Ursulo, but Adán did not hear the slightest sound; he was absorbed with his vigorous shoveling, digging into the indescribable substance of that terrestrial river, while Ursulo steered the rudder.

It was Ursulo's invitation for Adán to kill him. But the oars were burying Chonita and they covered her body with ashes.

Like tiny dots, like crosses, the names were repeated in Ursulo's head: Valentín, Gabriel, Natividad . . . the dead. "I wonder what he felt when they paid him for *my* death? He probably simply said: 'I'm going to kill Ursulo.' " He could imagine the callous emotion, the almost voluptuous masculinity, the soothing, dull animal sensation. Adán must have descended from animals. From Mexican animals. From the coyote. From the brown hairless and voiceless dog, the pre-Columbian *ixcuintle* with its body of shadow and smoke; from the serpent, from the snake; from the very sad and stonelike iguanas. If he had had a machete or a gun and if his daughter had not died today, Ursulo would have killed him. Because Adán was the child of animals, the pre-Columbian animals that had something religious, savage, mysterious, and cruel about them. Even though Ursulo descended from those same animals.

The river had become a wild horse wounded by burning metal, galloping out of its bed.

They could kill each other. Either one of them could give the signal, the death move. "All he or I would have to do would be to push," thought Ursulo, but a shriek restrained him:

"Ursulo!"

The desperate cry from Adán who had been hurled into the river by the blow of an oar.

He dove in as if something simple and harsh, like the marriage of two dark forces, had a hold on him.

"I've got to save him."

Ursulo fought desperately against that senseless body that grabbed onto him impeding his swimming. He was going to save him, God knows why. Perhaps because he would really be saving a kind of destiny represented by that man. That Adán, son of God, father of Abel, father of Cain; he would be saving the obscure fratricide; the crime of the Father, the Son and the Holy Ghost. Today he could not allow him to die. Any other day but today, when his daughter, back in his house, under the candles, was receiving her last light, the blinking gust of nothingness.

He threw the body into the bottom of the boat, his chest heaving, dark with a wet breathing, a wind blowing rapidly near exhaustion.

Why had he saved him? They were two voiceless, hairless, brown and solitary *ixcuintles*, frozen in a pre-Columbian frame, preceding the Discovery. They descended from death worship, from the old treks during which whole ages died generation after generation looking for the eagle and the serpent. They were two flintstones, stones capable of light and fire, but in the end pitiful stones, still vibrating from their ancient collision, from the time of the primitive steps of mysterious man, the first populator who had no origin.

They would cross the river and then, before reaching the priest, the strong mescal would burn their bodies, painfully warming them.

Yet what did all this mean when facing all that was dead, dead and without resurrection?

The night seemed without end and Adán, inside *La Cautibadora* as if in a coffin, with his dark intelligence and faltering breathing, was also without end.

The oars pounded the terrestrial, funereal water. "Thank you," thought Adán; but an inexplicable resentment, a shame, a resentful gratitude, prevented him from uttering a single word.

They could finally make out two or three flickering lights, which in their rising and falling announced the small village. The bells of the humble church released into the air their trembling, anguished notes, as if they were tiny twigs snapped off from a more solid and central branch. It seemed like a cry for help in the middle of the turbulent night. "Why didn't he let me drown?" An unexpected feeling grabbed hold of Adán's chest, and at that very instant he had wanted to fling himself on top of Ursulo and throw him into the river and free himself once and for all from everything that had anything to do with him: his hatred for him, his fear, his gratitude.

"I could kill you right now," he screamed; "but I don't want to."

Ursulo did not say a word, understanding that if Adán did not kill him it was only because his daughter, Ursulo's daughter, had died, and today they were going together for the priest.

II

The small, slightly apprehensive priest stared at the two men, at once so alike and so different, without understanding them. Eyeless Adán, his ugly face, his evasive stare, his stiff, brutal hair. Inscrutable, withdrawn Ursulo. Both men's lips had a way of expressing nothing; they were not sensuous, but at once both thick and beautiful. Just strong, sculptured mouths covering clenched teeth of corn. Eyeless. Eyes that could not really be seen because they were so sunken and thick: agile, dry, living, sharp stones, stones that could cut and also see at night, since their origin was in the night, and, more than eyes, they were a frozen shadow.

"We've come for you," said Adán with slithering indifference, his words full of apathy and coldness, like a silent threat.

The priest stared deeply at him. This man who came before him with his simplicity, his soft hardness and his exactitude, was a strange man. It was impossible to know him—and even according to hearsay he had become unreal, mythical—except as something vague and sinister. Nevertheless, he was gentle. Perhaps he killed with tenderness and affection because murder struck him as sensual and hot, and the blood's warmth just as necessary as the terrifying power to take a life.

As if surrendering to weariness, the priest and his wretched, vaguely pious soul were overcome by a debilitating anguish. He thought he ought to refuse. But at the very same time, the plea or perhaps command or whatever it was that Adán had meant with his "We've come for you" kept pounding in his heart. We've come. In order that he accompany them, in order that he go with them through the night.

Beyond the church's walls was the river, liquid sword, turbulence of shadows. Only a few days before it was a wretched, watery trickle of slow mud.

He wanted to refuse to go with them. The river had swollen. It must have rained a lot in the mountains yesterday or perhaps last week. And today, it was raining infinitely here in the plain, with no sign of letting up, a flood. It had gotten to be so dry that the animals, especially the dogs, had already begun to die of thirst.

He was just about to refuse: "Forgive me, my children," but the overwhelming simplicity of these imposing men who had emerged from the night blocked any effort to deny them. They were men of the night and men of death, and they were right there before him, reeking of mescal. But if he had said, "Forgive me, my children; I cannot," and followed it with some lame excuse, they would not have flinched, but would instead have simply murmured something like "It's all right, *padre*" or "It's okay" or "Please forgive us for bothering you," speaking with a steady, unemotional voice. And then they would have departed once again into the darkness, because their lives were determined by the shadow of a fixed thought in which things simply happened.

"I've got to accompany them," he finally thought, defeated by his own stupor and by the silent, obstinate force emanating from them.

He knew them only through hearsay. They were invulnerable, living, muted symbols with a tenacious passion running through their blood. "And," he thought, "if enemies such as these men have come together today, it is only because they have postponed their hatred and replaced it with that silent, somber coexistence of the nation." It was impossible to imagine that they had ever shaken hands with true loyalty or that the true meaning of Christ's words had ever been revealed to them with the warmth of its voice. "They do not believe only in Christ, but also in their own inanimate Christs, in their own formless gods." In these, a consubstantial and sorrowful Christ was leaning over the serpent inhaling its venom.

Adán's short, heavy body was breathing, and who knows what could have become of the oxygen that entered his nostrils and later mixed with the desolate, pathetic composition of his blood?

Invincible Adán, who muttered without the slightest trace of reproach:

"If you don't want to come, *padre*, don't come."

The priest looked down at his feet, without responding. Sorrowful feet that held up the corporal mass, that permitted it to stand upright. They were the feet that marched, moved, and roamed over the earth. Christ died with his feet nailed together, and those terrible words burst from his solitary chest: "Why have You forsaken me?" And when he called to Elijah the people believed for a moment that he really was the Son of Man and that God would appear to save him. In any case the mystery was performed and Christ was lost. He was lost because of the nails that bound him to the cross, to the world and to his quality of earthly, vulnerable man, with wounded feet and a sickly, unmiraculous will.

The priest now felt the nails in his feet. Indescribable carpentry of suffering and solitude. And facing his feet, the humble feet of Adán, and also of Ursulo.

He turned to look at the two men who had now become two Indian angels, fierce angels in threadbare shirts with both infinite nostalgia and deep dread. It would be absolutely impossible to do anything to hurt them! They looked as if they were in continuous formation, amassing and dispersing their own matter, absolutely defeated, but nevertheless a certain corner of their being remained stubbornly triumphant and hostile, paralyzing all enthusiasm. He imagined he saw in them only the human form of a very sad and resentful murmur. They were a muffled thud, a simple collision of objects without light.

He then imagined that they had been formed by a desperate animal, which was its own enemy and whose strength came from its own capacity for self-destruction, for not existing.

Adán was made of a thick, bleeding liturgy whose ritual was denial for denial's sake, a liturgy which had been born of a general expiration in which light was completely extinguished and on which they later built only destructive symbols, stones in whose foundations impotence germinated, becoming will, mode of being, and physical appearance. Adán was vigorous impotence, passionate indifference, and active apathy. He represented those snakes that kill themselves with Promethean rage when they are defeated; he represented everything that has poison and is immortal, totally humiliated, and slowly crawling.

And the sight of equally enigmatic Ursulo, with his distant shoulders sunken far below his vague, triangular head, also instilled fear and the certainty of suffering in the priest, the fear and certainty that something inevitable and evil was happening on this earth. "The dead are burying their dead," he thought absurdly, since the evangelical words were themselves absurd. "And," he said to himself, "as mysterious as these words are, where do they really come from?" He had not been able to respond, but the words were like an obscure and accurate definition. "The dead bury their dead in this country." He then remembered Christ's exact phrase when he was in Galilee, where he had arrived after having crossed the lands of Samaria, although the custom among the Jews was to cross it along the Jordan River. It was said in response to one of his disciples who was asking: "Lord, give me permission to go first to bury my father." Jesus then said strangely and profoundly, that mysterious and stunning phrase: "Follow me and let the dead bury their dead." The dead thereby acquired a living, superior quality. Consecrated and immortal, they became suddenly an attitude, salvation, resignation. And this country was a country of walking dead, a profound country in search of an anchor, a secret sustenance.

The priest felt depressed before the two men. Nevertheless, something powerful and incomprehensible tied him to them, as if they had opened a deep emptiness in his heart.

They were the feet and the nails. The incapacity for resurrection. Eli, Elias, the King, the Father, had abandoned them. The feet on the cross; the crossed feet and water and blood gushing from the flesh to inundate the immense country, blood and water made of stone.

"Get ready, *padre*, so we can leave!" said Adán. And it was curious that despite its imperative form the sentence had been uttered with some tenderness.

The priest heard that damp voice that actually seemed to contain tears, and his spirit filled with even greater enigmas. "In spite of everything"—meaning in spite of that tenderness, he thought with some difficulty—"this man has no religion," since he was witness to his open nakedness, and his lack of sorrow and mystery. It was a voice antedating paganism, associated with another mystery: nails of humble, dark flint piercing the feet of the wretched and tender Huizilopochtli. Another non-Catholic mystery of mourning and death.

"Is it very far?" he asked.

"On the other side of the river."

He expected that answer. He feared the river, the Deluge. He feared the elements. Fire and air.

"Do people still live there?" he then said with unintentionally insincere surprise.

He was not unaware that people lived on the other side of the river, but when today he was reminded of it he felt sorrow and a kind of remorse. He was no one or nothing to those people. Ever since the dam began to crack and the drought had arrived, they had been living over there like starving dogs. They lived obstinately, refusing to abandon the land.

Ursulo and Adán nodded.

"Very few, *padre*, only four families."

The priest moved his head. It was inconceivable to him that human beings could have remained in that solitude. He had conjured up an image of a miserly, barren land: long stretches of dry, pitiless limestone where horses' skulls flourished and the dry stirring of thirsty snakes could be heard; wretched land with only its cactus of ashes and the bitter juice of remote tears buried in a distant geology.

"That's where we live, *padre*," repeated Ursulo.

He said those words firmly yet with some grief, with his hardened lips, and his hardened soul thinking about the brutal persistence that had them bound to the useless land. They had waited long months for the rains, for their fertile and hopeful fall.

"Let's get going!" the priest then said, just as he finished getting ready, fearful and sorrowful.

The storm had increased its fury. Blue lightning burst from the clouds of coal and the sky appeared threatening.

The priest thought it was necessary to pray right there under the storm. He looked again at those feet now moving in the mud. Primordial, solid feet. On them stands the statue of man, but Jesus was also wounded in his *hands*. And from hands comes work, the sturdy hoe, the virile hammer. It was necessary to pray. In order to pray, he needed to moan and to speak, but his heart was in turmoil and his hands remained impotent beneath the enraged sea of heaven.

"Drink, *padre!*" Ursulo told him, handing him the bottle of mescal.

Mescal; vinegar. Because man is thirsty when he is near death. And he was then able to understand, with enlightening clarity, that those two beings and the hundreds and thousands who populated the contradictory land of Mexico, always drank their savage, impure alcohol, their bottle of sorrows, silently and lovingly when they were beside their dead.

He drank the mescal and the fiery drink slowly worked its way into the shadows that covered him, pounding with its metallic, hard scent.

Not far away, the river sounded like a giant, breathing lizard, and the twilight morning thrashed like a blind man from behind the stubborn clouds. Dawn would never arrive. The land had lost the morning; an agonizing struggle broke out between the storm and daybreak, between the giant saurian lizard of storm and the sword, similar to the beginning of this system of love and hate, animals and men, and gods and mountains that is the world.

Morning often spills its luminous blood softly down an atmospheric, angelic ladder, and valleys and hills and ravines fill up with its sonorous arrival, its multiple fire. But today, water and blood were running through the same vein, near the same rib, Christ of the air, repetition of the lance, and they only permitted the human twilight of a funeral shroud, subtly present, a somber blow from an inconceivably high and distant sky.

"No, dawn won't arrive," the priest thought. "Dawn will never arrive."

They walked silently beneath the storm. Adán's steps sounded firm, as if they belonged to the earth itself, and they were followed by Ursulo's steps and the more cautious steps of the priest.

There, on the other side of the river, would be Ursulo's wife, beside the corpse of pink stockings. Cecilia's eyes would be the same eyes by candlelight. The stockings, made of a humble Mexican fiber plant, the *popotillo*, were smooth and soft, although later, on her frozen legs, they would acquire such stiffness, solidity, and massiveness that he felt he could almost touch them.

Death had occurred, and it was so certain that it was almost incredible and nebulous.

Ursulo was sullen, totally resigned; nevertheless he wished his daughter were alive so he could hear her voice. That voice of tangible volume. Or even her breathing; even the brutal, desperate final breathing.

Adán's shadow cried out right in front of him:

"We're very close to the river."

But he was wrong; the river was raging, and it was only the crashing sounds of its waters that made it seem closer.

In front of Ursulo was his enemy's back. Death, which separated them, today bonded them with its silent truce. If the child were not dead and if Cecilia were not standing vigil over her tiny body, today's meeting would have been resolved in an instant. But that was impossible.

Carried away by a blind impulse:

"*Padre*!" Ursulo turned around, shouting: "Why don't you go back to your church?"

The priest said nothing from the darkness. His church was right there walking beside these men. His living church, not bound to a fixed place, beside that tender, bloody, and tragic Mexican death that came and went.

Ursulo himself understood that the priest could no longer go back, and not only because of the storm but, more important, because he was suddenly linked to what Ursulo, Adán, Cecilia, and Chonita represented: contradiction and despair.

The external landscape mirrored the landscape within them: desperate and contradictory. When the priest was saying "Dawn will never arrive" he was referring more to those hearts abandoned in the night than he was to the external world. To those trembling hearts of darkness of Adán and Ursulo. "And why," he asked himself, "am I going today with the sacraments?"

Ursulo and Adán were not of course what had called him. Something else was calling him: the shadows, the abyss, the sorrow, everything without dawn and without daybreak that was beating so strongly in the air, in his church, in the river, in the secret of confession. The landscape was the same, in the breast of each man and in history. That was why he was bringing the sacraments: to share the sinister revelation of the shipwreck, the permanent shipwreck in which they lived.

Those two men walking in front of him were his church, his church without faith or religion, but his profound and religious church. Religion had a strict, literal meaning for his church: re-ligare, to bind, to tie, to be reborn, to go back to one's origins, or to reach a destiny; but the tragedy was the fact that origin and destiny had already been lost and could no longer be found, and the men who were walking, the three men who were walking, two and three religious stones under the storm, were simply vocation and spirit without true purpose. Where were they going? To the dying or deceased child?

To the red and purple sacraments of Rome? Or simply to weep with the nostalgia of another distant, consubstantial death, common to all, because Chonita was simply one tiny accident of the earth, just some soft or stiff pink stockings?

He was what was conventionally called, when referring to a specific side in the religious war, a priest "of Rome." But the cardinal, papal, and irrevocable city meant nothing to the people. Rome was God and Rome was the Church. But here there was another God and another Church. The Christ of this land was a vengeful, bitter Christ. No one discovered, for example, a few years earlier during the Cristero War, that the national religion of *Cristo Rey*, Christ the King, was something different and that Rome, when preaching it and savagely practicing it with arms in its hands, had actually dissolved, fusing with what it had destroyed centuries before, when on the ruins of the indigenous temples it had erected its temples of hard, dry, inexorable and passionate Catholicism. The religion of the Cristeros was the true Church, made up of all the sorrow, bitterness, and misery of a people oppressed by men and superstition. They called themselves "Cristeros," accepting the name their own enemies had given them. And the harsh, brutal, and irreligious word gave them pride since it was in fact pregnant with strength and content. It was a kind of dialogue between mysticism and rage, between terror and cruelty. It was everything that had pushed man back to his ancient self where he used God to defend his right to shed blood and where with this blood he affirmed a vague, evil, and confused faith.

The armed struggle had broken out literally around the "Church" and not only in the religious, powerful sense of the word. There in the village the *agraristas* and *federales* had arrived, intending to dislodge the Cristeros, seizing the church and installing a dissident, schismatic priest. The priest "of Rome," the priest who today was accompanying Ursulo and

Adán, had observed the conflict from a safe distance. He now remembered the gestures and words and how those shouts of *"Viva Cristo Rey," "Viva la Iglesia Mexicana,"* and *"Viva la Revolución"* that both factions had hurled had absolutely no meaning whatsoever and were instead simply an audible record of the fury, fear, and unbearable desire to urinate and drink water that take place during a skirmish.

The Cristeros advanced cautiously, as if unreal, led by Guadalupe, their commander. "We are very few," thought the priest with great sorrow from his safe position, his lips totally dry. The shots were little white clouds and the men, seen from a distance, fell without a sound as if without suffering. "The strange thing," thought the priest, "is that we are fighting not only for the same building but for the same resentful, dark Church."

Because neither the Roman Church nor the Schismatic Church actually depended on Rome. Both were one and the same church, a church of nostalgia, resignation, and death.

From his vantage point the priest noticed Guadalupe waving his white shirt from the barrel of his rifle, asking for a cease-fire. He could hear the savage shouts of the conquering *agraristas* brandishing their rifles in the air under the brilliant morning. He did not know what to do. He fled. The sky was transparent; it was transparent and he was in crazed flight. "The same Church, yes, the same building." He was given shelter until dark, and then he left on horseback to hide. Days later he learned about the Adán he knew today. Cruel Adán who bore that name of a father. He learned about Adán: that he had murdered Guadalupe and tortured Valentín, another of the Cristero leaders.

Now, under the downpour, he was looking at that man's back and once again he was frightened; something was beginning to grow inside his heart. They were wide, heavy shoulders, like huge pyramid stones. His strong hips felt the effect of their weight and kept them balanced with a virile, steady pace. He felt him so very close, almost touching his incredible hardened-criminal nature. But a century of shadows separated Adán and the two men. It was impossible to do anything to him.

Adán stumbled on *La Cautibadora*, beached on the riverbank, and he uttered a shout no one could hear:

"We're here!"

He felt blind, overwhelmed, and the immense river with its infernal clamor pounded his insides.

"I only hope we can cross it," he shouted again.

No one heard him. No one could hear his own voice.

"It's going to flood," said Ursulo.

But it was useless to say anything under that nocturnal dawn and collapsed sky.

"Pray," thought the priest, "I'd like to pray." To beg forgiveness. To move to compassion with an obscure plea that strange will that was crushing the earth, because a monster was being born in his heart. To pray. But no. The figure of Adán made everything impossible.

"Let's go!" he said desperately.

Completely possessed by an immense roar, they pushed the boat, threw it onto the river, and entered the waters.

III

She was in fact wearing her pink stockings and a very pretty yellow dress. The mourners were admiring her there lying on top of the octagon-shaped soap crates covered with *crepe de Chine*, already somewhat grown, and with her tiny hands. They sat down again only to get up automatically and return to the yellow dress which was no longer breathing, which could no longer do anything.

Their prayers increasingly became a sleep-inducing murmur. They became terribly drowsy staring at those crates of soft wood printed with red and black letters and covered with the *crepe de Chine*. And then the mothlike sound produced by the wind. A moth that sometimes darkened the entire room whenever a gust of wind blew out the two candles.

The wind was like the river, delivering its moisture and its warnings, and the moth also had wings of water, like tears. The mourners were falling asleep with heavy eyes, but still repeating the same whispered prayers:

"Pray for us sinners, pray, pray."

Calixto and his wife, whom they called La Calixta, had been the first to arrive. Later Jerónimo Gutiérrez and his wife. They were all gaunt and ugly.

La Calixta looked pregnant, her thinness swollen with

dropsy; she therefore was quite remarkable looking, perhaps even more squalid. She also approached the tiny body and was not embarrassed to touch the stiff legs.

No one had brought flowers—Jerónimo had brought a bottle of tequila which he offered to everyone with his misty, gentle look—because their poverty was so severe and there were no flowers to be found anywhere.

They were startled in the beginning by the giant moth of the air, precisely because the darkness of the night predisposed one to fear and because the cracks in the walls seemed to weep as they whistled. The men began to drink tequila and a short while later the women too, with the exception of Cecilia, who remained in a corner absolutely silent.

"Just a sip," Jerónimo said to her, bottle in hand, "to keep you warm."

Cecilia stared at him so engrossed and so intensely that Jerónimo returned to his seat, clearly upset and frightened. "She seems insane," he said to himself.

The moth was monstrous, and the last time it had blown out the candles no one, because of laziness and a deep sense of fatalism, had made the slightest attempt to relight them, thereby confusing the room with the night itself, the animal night that prowled the earth. But everything was a return to the animal, and those beings surrounding the corpse only vaguely understood what was happening.

Cecilia got up to light the candles, but a gust of wind blew out the match, leaving behind only an instantaneous blue spark. She had heard so many things about corpses burned by candles falling on them! How their clothes had burned and then the corpses themselves, transforming death from its true frozen essence into a burning death of glowing embers. Burning death! Making the most of the darkness, she felt for her daughter's face, whose burning death was like San Anastasio's: "Enter me, death, and consume me with your tremendous fire which if it burns others in hell will burn me like heaven, to purify me. Enter me, torrid death." Her cheeks were more alive with that fire under her skin. There must have been some final thought left behind in her forehead, unreleased, hidden inside fiery marble.

When she relit the candles she found herself once again with the little stockings and the stiff yellow dress. She kissed the child's body to make sure of the heat of death. But no. Chonita was cold on the wings of the moth, and she was moving. Chonita was moving because death moves, advancing one millimeter per month or per year or per century. Under her skin her insides were moving toward their dissolution and the tissues were advancing and her hands were ceasing to be hands.

"Ursulo is taking a long time with the priest," muttered Calixto, who up until then had not uttered a word.

But their way of speaking was actually a kind of silence, and it had shrunk their voices to a monotonous hum.

La Calixta said that they ought to intone a eulogy. And all of them, so ugly and gaunt, agreed.

"Forgive us, *Dios mío*," they suddenly began.

It was a terrifying, unassuming song, full of terror before God. They sang with all their souls, remembering, intuiting an infinite punishment. If it had been possible they might have sacrificed a human being, cutting out his heart and offering it to the vengeful Divinity.

"Forgiveness and mercy."

Mercy for their lives without shelter, for their solitude, for their gaunt, ugly bodies.

"Forgiveness and mercy."

They were the dead, appearing before the tiny corpse, the frozen tribunal with its feet and lips and its yellow dress. There it was judging them from above. Limited and harsh, it was the scandal of death, brief in duration; it was the common denominator of those beings who had come together there to pray. When they looked at it they experienced a vague nostalgia and also the serious and at the same time pleasant presence of a profound and unknown thought. And they were there only because they were responding to a superior, tragic, noble, and somber destiny.

The moth was flying with its eyeless wings and outside was the night. It was a crawling snake, incessantly growing larger.

Death often took that form of unexpected reptile. It attacked without risk and grew larger only to leave its bite and retreat to its damp, dank corner. A snake with eyes so cold they were almost inexpressive, struggling in the grasp of the enraged eagle, the serpent and the eagle, both invincible in that eternal, frozen combat on the pitiful cactus of a people covered with spines.

"Forgiveness, oh *Dios Mío*; it grieves us a thousand times for having offended you."

Now it was stretching its coils and it was the river. Its cautious slithering could be heard on the stones, with the sound of liquid scales and aquatic skin.

"A thousand times our evilness grieves us."

As long as the tragic symbol of the serpent and the eagle, the tragic symbol of venom and rapacity, persisted, there would be no hope. This most atrocious symbol had been chosen to represent so perfectly and so pathetically this absurd nation, where the prickly pear with its bloody flowers was loyal and sad, its arms extended out over the water, a strange cross, timid, Indian and resigned.

Their voices, already somewhat hysterical because of the alcohol which had sharpened their emotions, grew louder, and suddenly the singers were releasing unrhythmic, primitive shouts, repeating the verses with desperate insistence. It was clear that they were half-drunk, with faces that showed no sorrow and exhibiting an imprecise and unsettling lewdness.

"Cecilia," stammered Jerónimo, drunk, "we are so very sorry."

And he immediately repeated, "very, very" in three different tones of voice.

Suddenly, as if those words were precisely what had been needed, everyone felt an inconceivable pity. Tears choked their throats and a mixture of feelings alternately beat in their breasts: sorrow, rage, sensuality, fear, and reckless, concealed lust.

"Yes, we're so very sorry, *Cecilita*," added Calixto, squeezing her hand concealing and defending his desire, while at the same time experiencing an impotent hatred for his wife's unusually large stomach.

La Calixta looked at him with her pitiful, repugnant, watery eyes, "The bastard," she thought with fear and tenderness. She had never had children, and her husband used to beat her on her swollen stomach so she would give birth. "You're pregnant by the devil," he used to tell her.

Cecilia pulled her hand away with indifference, but she did notice the muddy gleam in Calixto's eyes.

Once again the black moth flapped its stuttering wings and suddenly became a hard bird with dry wings, while the flames flickered. Chonita's face itself received a gust of wind and the candles went out. Then Cecilia got up and Calixto followed her to where he assumed the scaffold of crates to be.

She was going to light the candles but Calixto's right hand slid down her own until it took the box of matches away from her, preventing her from doing so. She felt his other hand rise from her waist up to her breast.

"Ursulo doesn't love you, *Cecilita*," she heard the calm, alcoholic voice over her shoulder.

The diminutive, *Cecilita*, was a word charged with desire, an imperative desire that wished to be powerful, all-powerful, capable of luring without fail.

"He doesn't love you," he insisted, squeezing.

Cecilia remained silent, without anger. Calixto's hand was between her breasts, trembling, while his heart pounded to break out of its corporeal structure to get to her. A long minute in the middle of the darkness had gone by and she was still finding it impossible to light the candles. The others, frightened by the silence, took up their monotonous singing, and then Calixto's voice was beside Cecilia joining the chorus, his hand still on the woman's breast:

"A thousand times, *Dios mío*."

And not with hypocrisy, because his voice was unintentionally trembling, and the words "Forgiveness, mercy, *Dios mío*" constituted another kind of yearning.

"I'm going to tell Ursulo," Cecilia whispered, making Calixto let go of her.

Then, with her wrist still trembling, she scratched the matches and transferred the violet light to the candles. She was trembling. She was trembling because of that revealing hand that had touched her no longer maternal breasts. Breasts that today grew free of the milky, sweet, vital thread which was once the living Chonita and which, now that she was dead, had broken her frozen, voiceless, and still little body.

Calixto looked silly in the middle of the room. His wife looked at him dazed, guessing what had happened during that minute of darkness. She was not jealous. She had not loved him for a long time now and, he, in turn, appeared never to have loved her. She felt almost broken, but in a simple, logical way, because the emptiness of life itself had been revealed to her in this night of death and profound desolation, and everything else had become meaningless there in front of Chonita's corpse placed thereafter in the middle of the night, in the middle of the storm, in the middle of oblivion.

Jerónimo, already drunk, was talking about the river, about how long Ursulo was taking, about a thousand things, with a monotonous, obstinate rhythm. His intoxication was total, as desperate, one might say, as all the intoxication of his people. A people on the point of abandoning everything, a suicidal and deaf people who were not only threatened with disappearance but who actually wanted to become lost and die despite the fact that their infinite compassion prevented them from doing so in gestures, words, savage and beloved revolutions, and in what majestically and gracefully came from their hands.

Totally drunk, Jerónimo was swaying with his reddened eyes, insisting on dire predictions that everyone would die, that the river waters would reach record heights, that it was necessary to flee. He stood up with some difficulty to look out the window:

"Everything will be flooded!" he shouted loudly, without totally understanding, because suddenly a great fury took possession of his being.

The rest of the mourners trembled upon discovering a certain threatening truth in Jerónimo's words. The serpent was going to expand without a doubt. Its liquid, crushing body would crawl the earth sweeping away all obstacles. It was already breathing and its pulse was spreading throughout the air.

For some reason, Jerónimo had wanted to hit his wife. He approached her slowly, zigzagging, and tried to look at her face but it was already too late; forgetting everything he fell to the ground, struck down by the alcohol.

"The bottle!" shouted Calixto when he saw the tequila spilling out of Jerónimo's pocket.

Little by little everyone had forgotten about the corpse. Perhaps even Cecilia herself had only a nebulous idea of her dead daughter, because she was looking at her with a very distant, very slow emotion, thinking stubbornly: "She's cold." But rather than being concrete, it was actually a vague, diluted thought. As if the iceblock of death had actually melted on the harsh, bitter, stonelike, resentful, and animal silent tears, ignorant—as it happened—of whether the corpse was burning, whether it was in flames or whether it was frozen stiff and numb.

She looked indifferently and without anger at Calixto as he devoutly picked up the bottle. His desire for Cecilia there next to death gave things an eerie content. It was therefore as if Chonita had not really died or as if she were not Cecilia's daughter but rather something foreign and even incorporeal.

"Ursulo won't be long with the priest," said Marcela, Jerónimo's wife, looking pitifully at the body of her husband lying on the ground.

They needed the priest to give them confidence, to purge them of their fear. With the priest near they would not be so frightened.

Because it was a fear. Fear perhaps of death. Not fear of their own death but rather of death in general, mistress of the night. The location of Ursulo's house probably had something to do with it, situated so far away from the others, although the other three were also very solitary amid the ruins of what had once been a town. Three or four inhabited houses in the middle of a wasteland.

Jerónimo's wife was trying to shake off her drowsiness and apprehensions. The room's opaque semitone, the soot-colored candles and the silent corpse made her sleepy.

What if the river really flooded? After everything that had happened in that land. First, the strike; then the failure of the system; and, immediately following that, the drought, as if the very earth were cursed!

"Wake up, Jerónimo, walk!" she pleaded, with a kind of rage, moving her husband with her foot. He opened his expressionless eyes and stared at his wife as if she were a stranger.

"Walk!" she repeated.

But Jerónimo returned to his position, sinking into a mortal sleep.

Calixto had sat down, the bottle between his legs and a stupefied stare on his face.

"Drink something, *Cecilita*!"

He was continuing to use with impunity the diminutive as an expression of his lewdness. A burning, trembling, sullen sensation ran through his body when he pronounced the word *Cecilita*, and he had wanted to press her hand in his once again or feel the maddening contact—the furious throbbing—of that woman's firm body.

"No. I don't want anything, Calixto," she answered very softly.

Now she was beginning to fear that man. She saw him as stubborn and impetuous as always, and even more stubborn in the darkness. Let Ursulo hurry up and get here.

The atmosphere was one of total loss and defeat, and the cold corpse, growing and walking on top of the soap crates, seemed like one of those specks left behind when a rapid train runs through the landscape. Let Ursulo be sober, not drunk, when he gets here.

"Let's pray a *padrenuestro* or something," muttered La Calixta totally dazed. She had not really wanted to pray, but she lacked the strength to do anything else.

"Yes, let's pray," Cecilia and Marcela responded simultaneously, but neither made any effort to begin.

A meager light was entering the room from outside, reaching the candles, wounding them. It was the morning light and it seemed as if the sun were slowly setting, like a bell tolling without peace.

A slight sacramental scent of candle wax and wool was already coming from the small corpse, the scent of an infinite church seeking its walls and the eternal void. Cecilia refused to endure this destruction, this thinning of the air, this dizziness, this difference and motionlessness of her heart, which was absolutely alien to what was happening, once again as if Chonita were not her daughter, once again as if no one had died.

She opened the door to go out into the wind and air, and she suddenly found herself alone, shaken, as if she were far away, many years away, and as if her leaving the house represented a journey of unexpected dimensions.

"*Dios mío*, how tired I am!"

All ties with the past had been broken. Her daughter of plaster was like the border cross that signals the last houses in the villages. In front of her there was only the storm.

"How terrible!" she said, thinking of Ursulo.

Obstinate Ursulo, full of stubbornness, who almost hated her. For what else could it be but hatred when he coldly forced himself on her with his obstinate, harsh love? For Ursulo, Cecilia was savagely his, as if it were a matter of life or death. His, like his own blood or his own head or the souls of his feet. He loved her as if he were someone perpetually dispossessed, landless and breadless; as if he were a fragile, barren tree. The love of a tree, of a cactus, of a thirsty, mortal vine.

She walked some steps away from the house, in the downpour. She could clearly see the steady running of the water. It was not singing; unlike the playful, dancing water of mountain streams, there was something hoarse and furious as it slid cunningly over the stones. What if Jerónimo were right and the river overflowed, demolishing everything?

With a silence so absolute and intense that Cecilia was on the verge of screaming, Calixto had come up behind her, squeezing her arm, his voice trembling:

"Don't scream," he said with an unreal, abstract voice. "I'm not going to hurt you."

His intoxication was evident, although a strange and logical lucidity, the possible product of his horribly taut soul, would appear to contradict that fact.

"Don't scream!" he insisted softly.

Cecilia pulled free from the hand that was pressing hers.

"I'm not going to scream."

Calixto gathered up his strength, speaking with a precise slowness. He did not notice his bare, disheveled head, nor his gaunt face. He appeared to be nothing more than a stumbling shadow, beaten by the rain.

"I love you, *Cecilita* . . . I've loved you for a long time now . . . not just today when you see me drunk."

Cecilia was not, in fact, unaware of this, but she knew it very imprecisely and unsurely. The absurd coexistence in that wasteland of abandon to which Ursulo condemned everyone was ultimately responsible for this passion. Responsible also were misery and suffering.

"It's impossible, Calixto," she said weakly.

Her resistance had never been so fragile. To feel that man's breath so close and not to be able to refuse him. Because the fact was that she was weak, weak of soul, and a sense of abandonment was further weakening her, causing her to feel pain throughout her body, drawing her close to sin.

"Go way, Calixto, please!"

He became suddenly timid. The unexpectedly free woman reversed his first impulses, frightening him. What had formerly been desire became suspicion and fear, since he did not know what he would have done if she had consented. What, in the middle of the storm and the river, watched over by the cold vigilance of the trembling, earthly, and living Chonita, as if death had spread a strange bond of love between them while at the same time opening up an unforeseen, cowardly road? "Go away!" he heard right up against his ears, and the words, far from being hostile, were actually rather close, encouraging, full of unsuspected intimacy.

"Here they come!" Cecilia said finally.

Two shadows were outlined against the house, backlighted. They were Ursulo and the priest who were entering the house where Chonita's small corpse slept. Their faces appeared to be tremendously exhausted, with sunken cheeks and a certain feverishness and confusion. The priest, however, in addition to being exhausted, had a startled, tortured look. He was contrite, and his eyes were a plea, a kind of unnamed charity, since he was feeling drowned, abandoned, afflicted by the memory of Adán. He was also saddened by these wretched mourners who had been brought together by their faith. Wretched souls who believed in his meager ability to save them.

"In the name of the Father, the Son and the Holy Spirit"; he mumbled the *de rigueur* oration with sadness and with an incessantly growing fear.

"Amen," Cecilia said to his back, entering with Calixto.

"So be it," she meant to say. So be death and resignation. So be the corpse and the suffering.

Ursulo turned to look at his wife with rabid resentment when he saw Calixto walking with her. He now obscurely understood the confused relations established between love and death or between hatred and death. It had been necessary that Chonita die for all this to happen. For Cecilia, like a black, desperate animal, to turn against him. But he did not dare do anything, although the glow in his eyes was emitting a dry, unsoothing blood.

The priest approached the corpse and touched its feet with the tips of his fingers wet with oil. He had been surprised because up until that moment he had thought that he would be attending someone still alive.

"I wasn't told that she had died," he mumbled.

"I forgot," apologized Ursulo.

Outside, the wind continued.

"Jesus, be not my judge but rather my savior."

The priest pronounced these words with a convinced soul, he himself as protagonist appearing before the jury.

"Attend to me in my last agony."

The last one, since everything was but a succession of agonies; and man was simply a dying being, on the road to death.

Jerónimo was beginning to wake up, still overwhelmed and still drunk. He straightened himself up somewhat, looked at the priest and his lips began to move as if they wished to say something.

"Get up, please," Marcela took advantage of the circumstances to beg him.

The snakelike hissing of the river intensified.

"No!" answered Jerónimo emphatically, awkwardly stiffening his head backward.

Calixto and Cecilia had sat down together, not far from the corpse. They were looking at Chonita expressionless as if they did not see her. She seemed very strange to them.

An impotent rage was seizing Ursulo. He needed to take revenge. Cecilia was finally prepared to abandon him. All the stored up resentment, the small hatreds of each morning, would soon come to the surface. Whatever existed before, including the intimacy, began to disappear from that moment on. Cecilia possessed a strength in the presence of which Ursulo realized his defeat. That strength had grown with Chonita's death and had liberated her; and Ursulo was no longer her master.

Jerónimo, from his corner, was flashing the wide-open, absent eyes of a drunk. He saw the priest there as an announcement of death and finality. What other explanation could there be? His presence could do no less than confirm the final abandonment, the last scene.

"The river!" he shouted as if he had suddenly remembered something.

Ursulo approached him with clenched fists. The river, yes, the catastrophe, but he did not want him to talk about it when he was about to conquer Cecilia for the first time, when he— powerful, lonely, and once again master of love—while everyone else was perishing, would be the last to die. Air from his own lungs, his blood, his breathing, his total anxiety, whatever, all this he would be able to give to Cecilia so they could both endure those last minutes.

"Shut up!" he shouted standing furious in front of Jerónimo.

And one could hear how death, in its watery form, was stalking around on the other side of the wall.

Ursulo turned toward the others:

"No one leaves here!"

La Calixta opened her eyes savagely:

"No one?"

In one sudden and senseless leap, she flung herself against the door, hurling herself into the storm. She disappeared immediately into the middle of the shadows.

Calixto, stupefied, could not understand what had happened; Jerónimo, insane and dulled by alcohol, understood even less. Ursulo barely took notice of her senseless flight. And where could the wretchedly poor and ugly Calixta go? Everyone would die, but La Calixta was to be the first.

Ursulo stared at Cecilia's eyes to see if he could find a new, returning spark. After all, they were going to die. To see if she would finally understand everything. To see if together in their expectation of death there could be future last moments for them to love each other fundamentally, as one can so seldomly in this world. "Forgive me, be mine," he thought, with all his strength, as if transforming his thought into an arm, into a will that could move the distant, anesthetized and inscrutable woman.

But Cecilia's eyes were harshly alien and belonged to no master.

IV

Marcela, Jerónimo's wife, helped wrap Chonita's corpse in a gray serape. A considerable amount of water had entered the room, and the grim rumble of the river outside was continuing its advance.

Everything was incomprehensible in that final moment in which they were preparing for flight, for that strange, senseless emigration. It is sometimes thought that to flee from death is to change places, to move far away from home, or to not resort regularly to memory; it cannot be understood that death is the body's shadow, the country itself, the nation, the shadow ahead or behind or beneath one's steps.

Those beings understood nevertheless that suddenly all of their destinies were united and that they were one and the same solid, dark entity, a sudden, unexpected community of ambitions, suffering, and hope. They were going to die together, beside one another, and this fact made them love instinctively this last relationship that was already uniting them, enclosing their eyes, hands, legs, and memory in one circle.

They wrapped the corpse in the serape and then Calixto tied it up with a thin rope. It was necessary to save it from death as well as perhaps to save everything else if possible — memories, objects — that remained there in the room.

Calixto was putting together a bundle of useless things, and in his exaggerated, clumsy drunkenness he began to see double.

At the foot of the bed, with the water up to his waist, like a seated corpse, Jerónimo, mortally pale, was breathing with difficulty.

"Get up!" shouted Ursulo angrily, kicking him with his foot.

The alcoholic corpse breathed heavily, motionless, becoming even more pale.

Ursulo and Calixto exchanged knowing looks.

"You'll have to carry him!" ordered Ursulo.

And then, by way of explanation:

"I'll carry Chonita."

They prepared themselves for the exodus, for the Biblical word that expresses the search for new lands. A word of hope, albeit remote, in the barbarous and encouraging books of the Old Testament, but cold and dead here in today's hopeless shipwreck.

Ursulo would carry Chonita and each of the others something else. Calixto stopped preparing his useless bundle.

But where were they going? They were already beginning to enter the final stage. Their lives now had only one terminal dimension. From this moment on, the minutes would merely be a preparation. Their remote past, rich or poor, would begin again in their memory: childhood, youth, suffering, desires, everything that had been their lives, from that day on would prepare itself for death.

Marcela turned to the priest:

"How can we be saved?"

The priest's eyes became more opaque. He replied with a vulgar theological comfort: strangely salvation had to be hoped for in something that we all carry inside ourselves, human compassion. Sarcastic words. The same words of the banished rebel angel: his own consolation, from his arrogant heart. And what other preparation could there be for such an anti-infernal death, when hell itself was the meaning of man, and heaven was inhuman, disheartening, still, and filled with base selfishness? "She spoke to me," thought the priest, "about how we could be saved, and I haven't been able to answer anything."

The insistent water outside was roaring, with mud, with roots. To die of water. Enemy water.

Cecilia went to her brown trunk. It was right to open the nostalgic belly of the trunk to see a little of the past. She had lost the future and without life ahead of her only objects of the past could bring together the blood that flowed, events. She went over the contents: the white, simple bodice, the old ivory fan, the straw jewelry box, the lock of her mother's hair.

To get to the trunk Cecilia walked from the bed to the dark corner, with the water up to her knees. The room now had a strange topography. Suddenly everything seemed unrecognizable and what had once been so familiar, like the hole next to the bed or the broken brick, were now under water, in communicative and visual contact with her foot, as if she were in someone else's house, not her own, not Cecilia's dry, sturdy house, but rather a nightmarish house, submerged and somberly aquatic.

The memories were beginning. She caressed the straw jewelry box resentfully with her grave hands. It was fragile to the touch, with its decorations.

These had been Ursulo's words:

"You belong to me totally. Physically, morally, spiritually. Whether whole or when you are ashes. Your bones are mine, your head, your teeth, your feet, your thoughts. You belong to me. You will always belong to me."

Dark Ursulo, who had subjugated because of his eagerness to possess completely. Possess everything completely: a shoe or an idea or a woman. He was dangerous, tormented, impoverished. Cecilia felt an infinite compassion before a heart so sad and furious, so filled with danger and tenderness.

"You belong to me completely, morally, spiritually."

He had spoken these barbarous words the morning they made love for the first time. Ursulo's bloodshot eyes looked almost criminal in contrast to the pureness of the sky. The fields were producing a monotonous, slow music; the air charged with light was as touchable as a wall.

She suddenly became very frightened upon understanding that such an enormous, limitless human love could only be felt by a solitary and disconsolate man, a pariah of the heart, a naked man. She then understood that in having yielded to Ursulo she had sealed an infinite pact.

It occurs sometimes that in a mysterious instant, in an inapprehensible flash of lightning, the spirit or instinct or the dark, unknown unconscious expresses its profound word. Then the truth without voice, without attitudes and without gestures, is bitterly revealed to us: the absence of love, loneliness, or irrevocable contempt and loathing.

Ursulo had discovered that message, but his pounding heart was furious and blind before the invisible enemy. He felt a strong desire to beat Cecilia because, in harming or wounding her, he could feel that she was his. But this was only fantasy, nothing showed on the surface; and they both found themselves together at that time in the grass, and under his strong arm she was indeed his.

"Cecilia, Cecilia!" he shouted like a madman.

Understanding the fate of his gloomy soul, Cecilia said a few words of comfort with pity and an unromantic tenderness.

They then headed for the village on the other side of the river.

The water was pouring from the dam through the canals with the playful manner of a young musician. They were visiting the noisy market which smelled of *mezclilla* cloth and percale, in the colorful little plaza in front of the church. There was a trace of charm in everything: a transcendent and profound charm in the copper-colored breath of the villagers, peasants, artisans, all of them mixed-blooded, with an inner grace, a slow sense of abandon. The little plaza filled with swallows and pink geraniums, so like the girls themselves in their green *rebozos* and brightly colored dresses.

Under the rectangular blanket shading the shop, they were selling little golden boxes, jewelry boxes.

"Do you want one?" asked Ursulo.

He took the jewelry box in his hands.

"It's pretty," he said with a curious gesture. Then he paid the asking price.

This was Ursulo, sad, vengeful. He turned to glare at Cecilia with his evil eyes; he was stubborn, made of stone.

"Yes, very pretty."

And without Cecilia being able to stop him, he suddenly crushed the beautiful box in his fist.

This was the instinctive act of a desolate man who has never possessed anything, the thirsty man who after drinking from the crystal clear spring hurls mud and filth into its waters.

Nevertheless, they purchased another jewelry box, the very same one that Cecilia was now resentfully and sorrowfully caressing.

Calixto had approached, splashing in the muddy water of the room, and he was looking at the objects over Cecilia's shoulder: the golden jewelry box, the bodice, the fan. His look became somewhat tender as soon as he smelled the nostalgic odor the open trunk was releasing, an odor superior to that other, vague, immaterial odor emanating from Chonita.

Weeks and months and years of fragrances, a memory of surprises.

"Give it to me!" he said, fondling the fan.

Now, for some reason, he felt strong enough to show some intimacy with her. In this way he anticipated the possession, warming the bond. Something new was surging out of the possibility of disaster, the rising waters, the deaf river, the storm: they were going to perish; they were going to disappear.

"I can't!" responded Cecilia.

Ursulo was somberly observing the scene. He was warming his dead daughter in his arms. He was no longer possessor of anything in life except that body, a body that was enigmatic, disconsolate nothingness itself.

"As a remembrance," insisted Calixto.

Ursulo understood that if they were no longer paying any attention to him it was because the end was near and he was disarmed before it. Because if everyone was disappearing, everyone would perish and he would disappear even more, he would perish more. That barely insinuated, barely beginning, vague relationship between his wife and Calixto would grow little by little, gradually, right before his own eyes, because Ursulo was dead and had found himself fallen into the abyss, without any real existence, ever since the river had begun to flood, ever since the water had risen to their knees. He wanted to beg, to plead that he not be harmed because he was so wretchedly poor, but he was unable to dare anything.

"Cecilia, take the child," was all he could mumble, and he held out the corpse.

Cecilia turned her head and looked with astonishment at Ursulo's aging face. In such a short period of time Ursulo had already become a dying man. She reached out her arms to receive the corpse, and as she brought it to her breast she experienced a strange sensation. Ursulo himself was being returned to her in Chonita's body, making her whole once again.

"Ursulo, *Dios mío!*" she broke into tears for the first time.

"It's her again."

For some reason, she was crying, and Ursulo noticed through the path of her tears the very path of his love and his return. She was crying and was not cold or hostile. When he touched her and drew her to his body or, more properly, to his truths, and when she had responded with eyes of weeping, reconciliation, and sacrifice, he had a feeling that all this was new and that she, right there beside him, was the beloved prodigal.

The priest was struggling to get Jerónimo to stand up.

"Get up!"

Get up, move, walk, look, die.

One must be saved for death. So death will not arrive senselessly but rather precisely, exactly, cleanly.

"Jerónimo!"

Ursulo approached to help and between the two of them they sat him on the bed with his feet dangling over the water.

Calixto was still staring at the objects in the trunk. There they were, motionless and sad, final possessions.

"As a remembrance, Cecilia, just as a remembrance."

As he persisted with his fondling of the fan, he was feeling an entire superstitious world of objects at his fingers: a piece of paper, he could not tell, but something filled with the gesture of giving, with the sweet, dreamlike, and loving act of giving.

Cecilia's impassive eyes, still cloudy from crying, returned:

"They're *my* memories."

No one could take them from her. Not even this death of this day that was about to destroy everything.

She was preparing herself to leave the earth as if walking in her sleep. Life abandons objects alongside the road as it runs its course: a book, a lock of hair. Touching her mother's hair today, Cecilia trembled strangely, as if she were touching something very delicate and sensitive within herself, something like the innermost palate or some internal organ. She remembered that she had been at the point of dying when she was still in her mother's womb, and, as she reflected on this, she felt a kind of a concavity, a strange relaxation. She could have died: her mother and father were fleeing through the mountains. She could have died as if she were inside a warm ship. Pregnant, heavy, bestial, her mother was unable to endure: she lay down under the trees, under nature. It was nature face to face with solitary man. It was what no one can understand until his solitary soul begins to vibrate next to mountains or vast meadows or infinite narrow paths, and one can finally see man's venture: the conquest of a mountain, the side-stepping of a precipice. His venture of victory over an unconscious enemy. But it was not the trees nor was it the ravines but rather men themselves who had pursued them, had found the couple and then given chase to the fugitive, Cecilia's father. They could have killed her mother as well, but those membranes, that thing that had not yet begun to breathe but was still feeding itself with tissue, that heart, that mystery, her body, Cecilia, holy Cecilia, had absolutely dismayed them, instilling in them the respect mixed with repugnance that a large pregnant stomach always provokes.

There was a memory in Cecilia, a tactile memory of the event, an almost vegetable memory of reflexive emotions such as fear, for example, or pain. Memory like lights drenched in blood, as if someone were pounding against her closed eyes. The prodigious mystery of the placenta and the noble umbilical cord.

"Give me the child," she heard Ursulo's voice behind her.

She handed over the corpse, the symbolic object, and once again she felt terribly separated from Ursulo. Once again she was leaving him alone, without shelter; once again she began to break what united them.

The corpse was a small parcel of clothing, a textile bundle of serape and cloth, a small yellow face, the protected, caressable, precious dead child, still so large. So large with its living death, in its death that had not yet died. And the napkin with which Marcela was wrapping some food—stiff tortillas, salt, dry beans—was a generous, colorful butterfly of the people which flew from her hand up to her shoulder. Tying it behind her thick shoulder blade, Marcela was then able to reach her husband.

She would have given her entire existence just to wake him. Just to have a single spark of light leave his eyes. She rubbed the drunkard's temples both very fiercely and very gently. "If he could only see me for one second, even though he would die afterward." But she was going to lose him.

Already senseless, Ursulo had the child and was pacing from side to side knee-deep in water, producing a deep sound resonant with movement. He stopped in front of Marcela.

"Let Calixto carry him. He's not going to wake up now," he whispered, glancing at the drunkard.

And without perceiving it, he had dictated Jerónimo's death sentence: "He's not going to wake up now." Marcela lowered her head. It was possible. Perhaps he would never wake up, not even to die. She grabbed Jerónimo's wrists violently shaking him. Let him wake up. Just once.

Outside, the water had become frenetic, the immense body of an infinite, thrashing serpent.

The priest had positioned himself in the middle of the room, where he had been whispering softly on and on, but as the roar of the storm grew louder he raised his tone, determined to triumph, to exorcise.

"My soul glorifies the Lord."

It was necessary to glorify him; to exalt with great irony his entire creation, since God was precisely what was taking place in their hearts, with everything that this included: tears and life; death and creation.

"He extended the arm of his power and obliterated the pride of the arrogant, upsetting their designs."

Senseless, audacious arrogance. The desire for immortality; the insanity of a life after death; the refusal to surrender; growing and struggling within the limits of a humble life, always ready to negate oneself and disappear, a life God had, for His own pleasure perhaps, made better by the sacrifice and total surrender of his children, all this had been crushed by "the arm of his power." This arm that was now crushing the pride of these people, this arm that was now knocking on the door.

The priest trembled when he realized what was happening to him: was he not also struggling to survive, struggling not to lose his life, a life that had merely been lent to him? Did there not also beat in his heart the arrogance of immortality, when as the captain of a ship he ought to be the last to be saved, the one to sink while the rest of the shipwreck victims made it to shore?

"He exalted His servant Israel . . . just as He had promised our fathers, Abraham, and all his descendants."

"Shut up, *padre*!" Ursulo pleaded, and the priest stopped talking immediately.

It was all so useless.

Cecilia remembered at that moment that there was an insane virgin inside her trunk among her precious things, and she was burning the arrogant oil of her lamp. And Cecilia did not want to lose this memory, this white bodice, stained with the red oil of a prodigal virginity. She guarded the bodice of her first love as a holy testimony. Her first love, before Ursulo.

The love of an intensely bright and brief morning. Ursulo's resentment had to do precisely with this first love. Deep inside Ursulo never forgave her for not having been his from the very beginning. There was therefore always the impression that Cecilia did not belong to him, that she was only on loan to him.

She still loved Natividad fervently. How could she not, given so much generous blood binding them: the abundant, primitive blood; the blood of surrender; the blood of the white bodice; and that blood of his, finally having come together in a decisive marriage ceremony. Blood. A ceremony performed in blood, that profound singing liquid. In spite of everything that had happened—the very first time they had met; the coarse, masculine directness with which Natividad always spoke to her; the five or six brief days they had lived together—she could only remember violently and uncontrollably that night when Adán and his people had riddled him with bullets while he slept. She had run out into the corral when she heard the shouts and shots. She had refused to believe what she finally understood had happened: Natividad completely dead, his eyes half-open, his lips without words, his blood thick. Then Cecilia ran, like a mad woman, in search of who knows what. She did not shed a single tear, and later the Syndicate carried Natividad to the cemetery on the other side of the river. They placed flags over his body, black or red, she could not remember. One year later Ursulo became her husband.

Calixto let go of the fan that he had requested as a remembrance, approaching Jerónimo to pick him up and carry him. They had to flee. They had to abandon the cursed land and river and find a hill, a promontory, salvation. Maybe the storm would end tomorrow and the warming sun would invent some hope. Calixto thought it curious and childish to have requested a remembrance from Cecilia precisely during those moments when everything—eyes, lips, kisses, blood, body, glances, thought, history—was going to disappear forever. And in the face of this singular, definitive fact, what could the past, however important or profound, matter now? "Now," he said to himself, "I'll have to carry that drunkard Jerónimo on my back." That is, Jerónimo was no longer a man but rather a symbol, and in any case he would die soon, probably without waking up. "Why should I carry him?" Calixto then noticed Marcela's anguished eyes, whose pupils flashed as they guessed at the self-interested thought that was moving behind Calixto's narrow, ungenerous forehead.

"Help me!" she cried weakly.

She was pleading timidly because she was still struck by Calixto's coldness and brutal indifference which had allowed his own wife to be lost without his making the slightest attempt to stop her. What could possibly matter now to Calixto when today darkness itself was pounding stronger than ever inside his sullen heart? Marcela trembled with fear and a strange feeling of compassion. Of all of them she was the one who was awaiting death with the most composure. She understood that she had to arrange this last day or week of life left to her as best she could, ripping from her heart everything that could tie her to the world. She had no questions, because she had never questioned herself, silently fulfilling instead the dictates of her warm, useful existence. Today everything was ending. The final act had begun, and if everyone had to die why not she too, with resignation and sweetness.

"Just help me. I'll carry him," she insisted before Calixto.

Calixto smiled somewhat ironically, pushing her aside.

They now began the exodus. They had tied themselves together around the waist with a rope so no one would be lost. Ursulo was at the front, his beloved bundled corpse in his arms.

The priest tried to say something; he turned around for the last time, opened his eyes and with a shaky voice, overcome with weeping, attempted to speak. But Ursulo's angry gesture stopped him cold. The priest trembled, his small eyes revealing his infinite affliction.

The shipwreck was beginning, under skies of solitude. They would walk without direction in the middle of that dark night of sunless morning, searching and hoping. Perhaps they would find a rock, some refuge, or perhaps death would suddenly surprise them, with water or a lightning bolt. But they would walk.

Without destination, without objective, without hope. Because they could not help themselves.

V

That is when a bird of paradise or a boat suddenly appears, and the tissues and cathedral of the brain, with its domes, take on shapes of weariness and surrender, and once again there is a strong hissing wind and plea inside, passing by silently and ceaselessly with the water of bays and blue lights. You loved once, maybe twice, you had children who suffered; there were also tears and work and sex. Things burst out of the body, sometimes magnificent silences, or a voice or semen or excrement. Feelings of closeness, greetings, walking around in the early dawn or faithful noon, transformed today into a monsoon inside the skull, toppling one final hope after another. First the hope of sanctuary, of a room with a mother and a face; then the hope of weeping, and then of oblivion. Not to suffer, for everything to be forgiven, for no one to cry out, closing their eyes with rage; for the persecution to end a hundred times, for a century. For there to be no one but one's own total solitude.

But weariness suddenly pounds; weariness and thought: walk, conquer all obstacles; let my heart go on, let it keep beating, let it still be a heart. This, when all is said, is what man is left with, what is finally his: pure rage, teeth, the fury of salvation.

"Ursulo!" Calixto shouted, stopping suddenly. "I'm not going to carry him!" As he spoke he slowly dropped Jerónimo's heavy body.

They must have walked a great distance, as far as the first tribe. Their chests were nearly bursting with heavy breathing and there was a nonstop pounding in their temples. The women, more bestial by the minute, were now only faithful, absolutely and terrifyingly faithful, breathing masses of resignation.

Ursulo stopped too, blind with hatred. He understood everything with brutal clarity. He understood that if Calixto was deserting Jerónimo's body, it was simply because what they all loved so much, life itself, was coming to an end right there. Calixto would also have deserted his mother and his children, because the struggle here was for no one but oneself. Ursulo understood this so clearly that he wound up asking himself: "Really, why doesn't Jerónimo die once and for all, and Marcela too?"

He turned, his face distorted by anger:

"You don't want to carry him?"

Jerónimo had his face in the water, awkwardly bent over and in danger of drowning at any second.

Ursulo had wanted to kill Calixto right there, but it would have been impossible. Chonita, and now Cecilia too, held him back like chains. Chonita's body was made of chain, of iron. And his wife was like a thick anchor amid the shadows which had been lowered to the very depths, already immaterial. Ursulo would lose everything by killing Calixto, and first of all Cecilia, forever.

"You are a son of a whore," he limited himself to saying, with clenched teeth.

He gave Chonita's corpse to Marcela, and shaking Jerónimo's body he hoisted him onto his back to continue the march.

Marcela saw how they were carrying her husband and she was right behind them, stumbling, strangely moved. Jerónimo was still breathing and this magnificent fact resonated in Marcela's gut like a tepid message and a promise. Jerónimo was not yet a corpse although he actually already was, so removed was he from everything; Marcela experienced a deep rupturing and an infinite desire, a kind of longing. Just as Jerónimo's voice and words had expressed earlier? Just as did his now flushed face? Sleep was already severing ties with all prior relations; it was the birth of death, the birth of the fountain that springs new and eternal, nothing else having existed before, and here in death without past everything was being created precisely in order to perish as well. And it was impossible for Marcela to use memory to reconstruct her beloved husband, because a wave of suffering and misery was raising an obstacle. She would never see him again with his former face, with his living eyes; all there was of him were his hanging legs and wretched, uninhabited shoes, kicking against Ursulo's solid torso. Please let him wake up from his sleep, from his surrender, and let his lips say something that would prove that he was not already dead, dead.

It was a drunken reveling of death from which he would never escape. And, in fact, who can show the fine line between life and death, the invisible frontier? Man dies so much when his mind becomes dull and distant. He dies from dying on his body where enigmas trample, and it is both easy and difficult to put an end to his strong, weak, demoniacal, celestial, intimate, old, and strange life.

A sense of emptiness and sadness crept into Marcela through her pores, then into the lower half of her body, through her toes and muscles chilled by the water. It was a disconsolate and infinite feeling where absolutely nothing existed, not even weight, and everything resembled a lifeless hand. Weightless Jerónimo on top of her, without Marcela feeling the caress of his gravity on her thorax or the sadness of his breathing on her cheek. Jerónimo, dead before death, alcohol running through his veins, and his widow, Marcela, walking behind, the tearful widow, in tears, in heaven, with huge, immense eyes like vaults filled with salt and eternal water.

"Give him to me," she begged Ursulo. "You carry Chonita."

Ursulo turned toward her, surprised and attentive. "Actually," he thought, "she should carry him, just as I should carry Chonita." Everyone was going to die anyway, and were it not for their burning, foolish desire for salvation, they would have just remained there, sitting and waiting, doing nothing. Why go on struggling? Did they truly want to live or was it just their terrifying, pointless obstinacy? Let Marcela carry the living corpse of her Jerónimo. A wind thicker and worse than that of the storm was blowing inside his skull, in furious grief along the plains of his soul. Let her carry her own corpse, her totally drunk husband, the wretched dead man on her back, until the end of the world, because vegetation no longer grew in his heart.

Cecilia held Chonita's body in her arms while Ursulo unloaded the drunkard onto Marcela's back. Marcela cut a grotesque figure with her husband. She was limping sluggishly, her legs wide apart, and she resembled a strange, prehistoric animal with something of a woman about it, a bloody, ugly woman, with its humpback, its pyramid, like those camels on whose thick, calloused hide grow weeds and plants.

It was absolutely essential that they keep walking now that they had no place to stay. That they keep walking intensely, but without a goal, in flight. Perhaps this infinite flight had to do with fate and not with them. But they were fleeing while still remaining, while still feeling the extremely violent longing to remain, for their flight was actually a search, and the desire to find a vital piece of earth on which they could be safe. That explains why today they felt unconsciously united, in transcendent solidarity against something that had not yet reached them, bonded together until their disappearance, in spite of the fact that they no longer had eyes and barely any spirit. They were ignorant of everything and mostly of themselves: whether they had a future, whether something awaited them later. At most, they vaguely knew about their own existences, always doubting whether there were other men and other countries in the world or other regions in their own country. Where were they going? Where, when the earth was probably completely flooded, from those remote foreign city-state names to the new-world names of Catholic saints, and finally to the sad dusty name of some indigenous deity? But, in any case, they had to keep walking, in search of themselves, because even though they might be defeated something deep inside was whispering to them that salvation existed, and if not for them then for that deafness and sorrow so filled with hope that they represented.

Ursulo was driving himself on with his desperate, superhuman will, trying to save himself, with the demon of salvation inside him repeatedly urging him on. Not to save himself from death but to save his own meaning and despair.

They were indeed going to disappear forever, as were the entire region and the country and the world. But those steps, that searching, would go on for centuries, in the wind, whenever someone paused long enough to listen to the voice of the dust.

On occasion it is discovered that there is a death that occurs quite some time after true death, just as life itself, in turn, begins quite some time before the consciousness of life. What remains of a human being during these rare, illuminating moments is something very similar to stone, stone breathing with the beginning of an ancestral idea or divination. These are the moments of the prodigy of the species, when the memory of the whole man can be seen in the lonely man beaten down by the revelation. It is discovered that in the beginning there was the inanimate, the crowd lying at rest and still cold, and a painful memory reminds man of his condition of silica or marble.

I was silica, and something so very distant, the essence of darkness, was inside me, placing me within the kingdom of the living, something immeasurable and incomprehensible, and fainter than the faintest whisper of presentiment. My motionless, dead atoms were preparing to outline a vertebrae; to arrive at the prodigious miracle of respiration under the sea, from where we would be born. The miracle had been necessary and my fate would turn me into a fish, a reptile, a bird, and finally into what I am today, weeping, eternally weeping.

Ursulo suddenly discovered that his kingdom was not of this world. That he belonged to the prevegetable world of the inanimate, and that like the first maternal stone he was merely an extrahuman will-toward-being, the most vehement, burning will of history, the will and vocation of stone: weaponless, thoughtless, motionless, and final, like stone, but waiting for a century, like a part of the very thickness of time itself.

His mother had died at childbirth, and an ancient legend of the country told of the indigenous goddess who from heaven had given birth to an obsidian dagger. The first human couple had been born from the smashed black and shiny splinters of this dagger, and from the first the second was born, and from the second the third, up until today. Abraham begat Isaac, Isaac begat Jacob, Jacob begat Judas and his brothers. Ursulo was the son of the obsidian dagger, and his mother was the goddess herself, a young goddess.

Strange that she was simply called Antonia, with no other name. Simply Antonia, like an animal that seems to come from nowhere. Antonia because she was an Indian, something evidently like an animal since she did not even know Spanish.

People gave her food with considerable compassion because Antonia was a kind of solitary migrant worker, far from her homeland.

She was a goddess with her dark, profound flesh.

Her parents, silent like her, lived during the times of the local boss Tatebiate, later killed by the government.

"*Señor* don Porfirio is sending troops against us," Tatebiate once warned all the men of his community. "We have to fight because he wants to take our river, our corn and our children away from us. Is that justice?"

Antonia's father spoke with his wife:

"Why does *Señor* don Porfirio bear such ill will toward us?" he asked. He was restless and profoundly surprised by what was happening. "He wants to take my children away from me. I'm telling you because I'm going off to war."

Antonia's mother calmly watched her husband leave.

"Kill *Señor* don Porfirio," she told him, and she returned to her shack to stop her year-old son from eating dirt.

"Where's my father going?" asked Antonia.

The woman's face became severe, absolutely convinced, and she looked at her daughter with profound eyes and without answering.

Antonia was ten years old when Tatebiate's men were defeated and more than half were killed. It made no difference, since they would be resurrected. But the *pelones* [federal troops with short-cropped hair] came to carry the families far away by order of the supreme government.

They led them to the railroad station.

"You're going to Quintana Roo," the government men said, "to work."

It meant abandoning the land, leaving everything.

Antonia's mother gestured somberly. The slow train approached like a fiery beast.

"We won't go, it's better to die," said Antonia's mother, and grabbing her year-old son by the feet she smashed him to death against the railroad tracks.

"You are a viper, you Indian bitch!" exclaimed a soldier as he ripped through her with his bayonet.

Antonia was left alone and later she fled through the mountain with a group of about twenty pursued Indians, grieving because they had lost the war. Perhaps victory had not been made for them, since for so many centuries they had had nothing and had been so poor. They began to fall ill and die.

Hungry and exhausted after walking many miles, Antonia arrived at the hacienda to be given something to eat. "*La Abeja*" was at that time a great hacienda, with thousands of heads of cattle, and don Vicente was a real Spanish *señor* just like his ancient *conquistador* grandparents. Antonia stared resentfully and speechlessly at all the people of the hacienda: the steward, the peons, don Vicente. She could not erase the image of her mother smashing the child against the train tracks.

Antonia's existence was surrounded by death, made for death. Should she live or would it be better for her to die once and for all, without a trace, forever? She was unable to find the words to ask for bread from the whites.

"Don't you know how to speak?" they asked her.

Then, looking at one another:

"No, she doesn't know; she's pure Indian."

She was a goddess about to give birth to her black, gleaming, obsidian dagger. She arrived there mute, simply fulfilling her destiny. Was it not right that she go to them so that everything might be fulfilled? She had been made for death:

the death of her loved ones, the death of her time; and something fatal and resigned was making her wait for it.

They gave her something to eat and she remained on the hacienda, without a definite job, working here and there, never speaking since she never learned Spanish.

"The only thing she knows how to say is *tortilla*," the people would say.

She was a surly, solitary goddess.

Don Vicente gently took her by her head, and then by her shoulders. Her ancestors had already said that "this land was to be possessed by the children of the Sun." Antonia received with resignation the seed with which her gods had died.

When Antonia died on St. Ursulo's day, the obsidian dagger bursting from her womb, don Vicente made arrangements for her burial and he carried the child off to the Casa Grande, to educate him.

Fourteen years later, while night was falling on "*La Abeja*," Ursulo saw don Vicente decomposed and hanging from a tree. That man was his father, but a hard emotion tightened his chest: "It's all right," he said, his heart feeling like a dagger incapable of love, he, son of the first knife.

The revolutionaries had passed through the hacienda the day before.

He understood today, now facing his own death, that this was truly not his kingdom. That he was very far from the world of men: isolated, extraterrestrial, the son of a goddess. His hollow, vanquished kingdom was not to be seen. There were ruins on all sides; and there was a thirst: stone that aspires to imponderable vertebrae, fish, reptile, bird, tree. Immense, buried mother stone. Obscure Genesis.

He heard a moan behind him.

"Help me; I can't go on!"

It was Marcela, with Jerónimo.

Ursulo stared indifferently:

"Let him die!"

Why carry him any longer? The sky remained dark and negative. Nowhere could a ray of hope be noticed.

"Leave him!"

Marcela was not wounded by Ursulo's selfishness. She almost understood him in that strange moment. She herself was touched by the ignoble, base poison of death. Leave Jerónimo, yes, to drown.

The group had come to a halt and the two women were holding up the drunk's body. It was not wrong to leave him there but rather very natural, even logical. Because death is like a cold, pitiless hurricane inside the skull. It shakes the trees where thoughts used to pass, and now the primitive, terrorized species reigns once more. All they had to do was let go of Jerónimo and let him fall face down into the water. He would simply stop breathing, filling himself slowly.

But what were they all doing there, without purpose, like sleepwalkers? They were, in fact, sleeping, dreaming what they were feeling. Wheat, a countryside seeded with wheat and the air brandishing its stalks. The sky behind them, immense and vast, more celestial the more it was dreamed. Clouds. Fraternal clouds moving under the dome with some demigod inside who was probably sleeping. The houses of the village, during those times in which people still had work.

Why not move and continue with the exodus? Yes, go on walking. How could they stop their march one single instant?

"Leave Jerónimo!" said Cecilia. "Let's go, for God's sake!"

Hers had been the only voice missing. Missing was her testimony of selfishness and hate. They would die beginning with that precise moment in which Cecilia had given this signal.

To continue, to fight for the last time, to make the last effort. But something was holding their feet to the earth. The nails, once again, of Christ.

Suddenly, a miracle: Jerónimo strongly shook himself free of the women, and he grotesquely and comically took several long strides, only to stumble and fall. He had died a few seconds earlier.

His death agony was immense and terrifying: first, in the house, before Chonita's corpse. Chonita was on her knees somehow praying over her own body. "My soul glorifies the Lord and my spirit is filled with joy." Jerónimo had wanted to put a stop to that kind of sacrilege where a twisted rag doll corpse was praying to itself. But it was impossible to speak, because cement was surrounding his lips and in the store someone was pouring the mescal into the bottle with a funnel. One litre, two litres, three litres, four litres. If the river was rising and had broken its banks, as in the Bible, flooding without end. "For the cold, Cecilia." Then blue flames rose from the soles of Chonita's feet, which had been soaked with oil so they would burn. Jerónimo wanted to beg them not to abandon him, because he was alone and dead, and he would not be able to roam the earth later without friends, without family. No. No more alcohol. His promise was firm. Let them put a stop to that river of alcohol where his eyes burned him as if Chonita's burning feet were inside them. "My soul glorifies the Lord." He had completely forgotten how to walk; it was as if he had just been born. When he tried to walk he stumbled pathetically, but not on the ground. Instead, he fell beyond the ground, into soft, terrestrial, asphyxiating clouds. His heart was no longer beating. What was pounding was a patriotic parade, there in the plaza of his village, at the head of which marched Chonita and Ursulo, who had been bizarrely joined together, Chonita sunken into her father's throat while he was making some kind of a noise. "*You* carry him!" he heard a metallic, nonhuman voice. "They're referring to me," he thought. He then began to cry with all his soul, because he did not want to leave his friends: good Cecilia whom he had loved so in life; Calixto, with whom he sometimes had a drink; Ursulo. They had all been so good to him! He tried to say something, to protest, but they carried him by force across a world on a journey that lasted 500 years. Afterward, now an old man, Jerónimo returned, and then it was that, in the mere fraction of a thousandth of a second, an untimely, magnificent lucidity suddenly formed in his brain.

"Leave Jerónimo," he heard Cecilia's voice. "Let's go, for God's sake!"

Yes, it was Cecilia's voice. She also wanted them to abandon him. Then the shadows came and it must have been at that very instant that Jerónimo, already dead, took a few long, ridiculous strides.

When they saw Jerónimo fall, everyone sighed with relief. Happily he had died.

VI

He tried to say something but Ursulo's rage restrained him. He appeared to be telling him to stop talking, ordering him to die. "That's precisely it," he thought, "when I myself . . . " But, in the end, it no longer mattered. He stopped and gently untied the rope that connected him to the others and with which they were trying not to lose one another. Unable to see a thing and surrounded by the storm clouds, a celestial shipwreck victim, he sensed how everyone was disappearing without noticing his absence. Then, on his knees and the raging water above his waist, the Christian words of resignation unintentionally came to his lips:

"All has been consummated."

The man now surrendering to death, on his knees upon the timeless deck, was not a ship captain. He was a human sinner, antiheroic, overcome by evil, forever defeated, his head having fallen into the deepest affliction and sorrow.

Where, how, on what demonic roads had he committed his great mistake? He had very little time to live. Just some empty and useless minutes or hours of desperate anguish. Because it so happened that since he was close to death the monstrous sterility of existence was being revealed to him, an existence whose objectives now appeared to him to be absolutely meaningless. His entire past had been a sad mistake without the slightest moment of victory.

As he touched his chest, he felt the dryness of his soul on his hand. A soul walled in by infinite circles, from one to a thousand, from a thousand to a million, with no internal light, with an atrocious darkness that permitted neither seeing nor breathing. It was terrifying to fully comprehend his defeat, and his satanic intelligence was repeating the undeniable truth: his walled, lightless soul had passed through life uselessly, sterilely, as if in a desert, leaving behind neither trace, branch, shadow, nor shelter. His mission had been to conquer. Everyone had this same profound goal: to conquer. But how, today, in his fleshless hands from which no plant or fountain or tear could be made?

The priest hid his face, pressing into his jaws, forehead, and cheeks with his fingers which had turned into claws.

"All has been consummated, lost."

Had he ever conquered what must be conquered in order to be productive and great? In order to be great even within the pure, angelic smallness of life?

He felt how little by little he was turning into stone, and the feeling was moving him deeply because it was true. The soles of his feet first, like sheets of stone, like funeral coffin litters.

What was the Good? he thought. The Good consisted of men having to weep and tremble from their very hearts, hearts they would see to be made of afflicted, animal fury.

Were the Commandments the Good? Or were they monstrous because they were based on everything man can never do? To love God above all things. And where was God? Let the entire earth stir until it becomes dust and Infinity is shattered. God, God! Where was He? From door to door, looking for God, with no answer. Along roads, in cities and villages, in the endless plains—no one. You will love Him above all things. Above your mother, your wife, your son, your brother, because what you truly love is your suffering, the tears you shed, your guts slowly rotting inside you.

Tears moving with their feet of permanent rain, deepening man's course like a river.

It had happened in Oaxaca many years before. He was studying that day at the Conciliar Seminary and that afternoon there was to be a meeting of the students in the choir of Santo Domingo, a beautiful church, one of the most active in the region, with stones that seemed to be anticipating the Resurrection. There, in the porch under its arches, one indeed felt the presentiment that death was simply one of life's required stations and that one would wake up afterward, no longer as a human being but rather as a cloud, river, piece of paper, ocean. The grave figures of priests, warriors, and monarchs, splitting up into a tree, into a hard branch of the great fertile and supernatural corpse lying there like burning soil, were like frozen time, like a fulfillment of life. All this had never died and the church was like an unextinguishable, living voice.

Possessed by this confusing impression, he climbed up to the choir. But before he arrived he was stopped by a strange song. He heard a falsetto song coming from the staircase, a savage song broken by continuous disharmonies. The notes spread out over the face of the earth, as if the voice were produced by an inconceivable vegetable throat of thorns and bitter juice, as if it were joined by the voice of the humble and aggressive wild *chicayotl* gourd, or as if it were the voice of the wounding cactus of a wasteland. That dissonant, elementary voice was certainly the plant of thorns sprouting everywhere, ashamed of its poverty and ugliness, fighting for goodness and beauty with its white flowers that no one would ever desire. And pleas, tears, sorrow, despair, absolute solitude, wretchedness, all this came together in that voice as if at the same time it possessed something of a weeping animal.

"Who could it be?" he asked himself, tiptoeing up the stairs so as not to interrupt.

But when he poked his head into the choir there was nobody there, not even his fellow seminarians. There were only the decapitated statues of the Martyrs, sculptured with a kind of distorted realism, alive in spite of being dead, looking at God from the floor where their heads rolled.

In spite of decapitation, those martyrs filled with terrifying pleading had not died. With their eyes open, and with a calm terror, they observed their blood bursting from their throats in a perpetual flow.

When he looked down into the nave of the church he noticed a man on his knees at the railing, his arms crossed. The off-tune, monorhythmic voice was coming from that man, the voice sad like the whistling of an earthenware flute. But it was not a song. The man was weeping on his knees, his arms crossed, with his cotton pants and frayed blanket. He wept in his Zapoteca language ancient tears. "*Patroncito*," he said in Spanish and then switched into the language of his people. "*Patroncito*" but it was not clear what he was begging for.

The seminarian had failed to understand anything at that moment, and now, after so many years, a bilingual voice was translating the Zapotecan words for him:

Patroncito: there are so many tears. Nothing but tears, Patroncito. My people fall ill and die. My wife cries. My children cry. I am crying so you can see me.

On his knees, there on the rock of the church, at the railing. On the rock, not on the railing.

Some tourists who were admiring the church stopped to look at the Indian with both repulsion and satisfaction drawn on their faces. "Poor man," they perhaps thought, "very poor. But this is a typical, genuine feeling." And they would point out: "in Mexico the Indians cry before white images, lamenting in their own native language. They believe that God is Quetzalcoatl, and that he'll come to redeem them."

God, always God. To what kind of sad, powerless god was this wretched Indian praying? No. He had no gods. Not even God. Only suffering.

The seminarian had then left the choir and walked out of church with his first doubt nailed to his breast. "You will love Him above all things." And what roads should one travel? And with what tools of love, if love was a feeling denied man?

Yes, the soles of his feet, soles of stone. Today he was no longer able to feel his feet which had become a testimonial, like a grave. He would soon have totally turned into stone, a collapsed pillar, and with the water climbing, it was only a matter of waiting, already defeated, without a moment of victory: he had not triumphed in the very first, fundamental commandment, God, because now he saw that he would never be able to believe nor ever to love Him above all things.

What was the Good, then? It was the capacity for horror before the abyss itself; it was sorrow; it was the powerlessness to expel inalienable evil from the soul. It was feeling the suffering of not being able to solve anything and the suffering produced by the fact that man is a small leaf, with a trickle of sap, like an inconsequential lament in the middle of the shrieking earth.

"You will love your neighbor." And why will you not despise your neighbor as you do yourself? Because all of life is the accumulation of contempts until the arrival of the final contempt, the great contempt that is death. And the minute of terror in which the unbearable revelation is heard is painful like a blinding flame: you never loved, instead you were contemptuous in all your actions: when you were fighting for riches or glory or when you actually believed you were working for your fellow man. And man does not hear this voice except for one second before, when it is no longer possible to go back and begin again.

One starless, peaceful night, he was startled by some steps outside his room in the village's small church.

It was one of those nights they talk about as being so enigmatic and solemn, when the sky shows itself to be empty and one can ask about the mystery surrounding all things: the small, invisible branch shaking in the wind; the dense abandonment of space; a shelterless, human star; a terrified planet.

After the steps, a voice on the other side of the door: he wanted to be let in, it was important. He could not see the window in the totally starless night, and the voice was right there.

The priest lit the lamp and when he opened the door the man was silent, the man with that voice, with eyes, and with hair as black as a brief shower of ink. He wanted to confess and that was why he had crossed the deserted nave of the church to get to the priest's room, the nave, the ship with saints and walls. It was the confession of only one wretched sin.

The Prince had bitten his lamb, he said, and when he said it there was a certain lucidity in his eyes as if he had discovered an unknown world. Because that was where he was beginning his confession and The Prince turned out to be the dog that had bitten a sheep. Prince with his mutilated tail and hard skin, beaten down with guilt, timidly waiting for his master.

He begged for forgiveness but his master was in a state of pure rage, his stick in the air, a savage sinner.

The man was confessing with his frayed clothing and he resembled a soiled redeemer right there before the priest; he was like a redeemer. Was this not proof that as we travel through life suddenly Jesus appears crucified in a brother, in a friend, in a woman, in the blood of a painful wound, in an animal?

He beat The Prince, knocking out one of his eyes and breaking his back with a stick. Then he left, the bloody club resting on his shoulder, while The Prince remained behind, with a death rattle.

"And imagine my surprise when I see that the little animal gets up as if blind and comes up to me to kiss my feet? That dog, *padre*, isn't that Him?"

The man disappeared into the starless night. It was a profound night.

As he remembered all this, the priest felt the stone spread through his body. It was now not only his feet or his soles. His knees were changing now, hurting him like a dagger thrust into the harmony of his bones. His piousness had died, because that is precisely where the joint of piousness resides, in one's knees.

The water was continuing to rise and its rapid current was already hurting his chest. He was going to die soon and he still did not know, he still was ignorant of The Good.

A priestly vow had upset his existence so that there he would perhaps find The Good.

On one occasion he was called to administer the last sacramental rites to a woman dying on the outskirts of the town. It had all happened so suddenly that he was not accompanied by his assistant, a wretched soul named Timoteo. Why did he go alone? This was one of the mysteries of his own soul that most disturbed him, causing him to deny God. Because if man, despite his will that can sometimes approach sheer terror, is denied God, and the conquering, absolute shadows become more powerful, why God? Why, if he were simply a blind, impassive entity? He remembered the temptations of Teresa de Jesus and how the Saint described that fire which was so immediate and threatening. Was it not an act of surrender simply to narrate the temptation and put the unerasable seed of memory once again in the soul? Teresa de Avila suffered precisely because of that fire, and one could notice in her memoirs her ecstasy in reproducing the temptation, as if there were voluptuous sensuality in repentance and The Good. And the victory over the devil had meant at the same time a pleasant albeit not divine relationship, precisely a concrete pleasure of the body and the flesh.

The priest arrived at the house where he was to administer the sacrament.

The woman was not exactly dying. She was going to die, yes, and thus she found herself to be in that obscene state which is the presentiment of death, her eyes shining and painless. She was suffering from leprosy and after a severe attack had asked for a priest to be called.

The walls of the room were almost bare except for the picture of the Virgin of Guadalupe, her hands in the form of twin doves that had been joined together, her brown skin, brown doves, her humble downcast face, unlike the painting of the Dolorosa Virgin in his church, painted by someone in the eighteenth century and whose cloth was already peeling off revealing an antiquated ochre canvas, a virgin who looked up toward heaven with anguish, her body pierced with daggers. The Mexican Virgin looked not up but down, her feet resting on a new moon held up by two small angels, her starred blue robe flowing among the clouds.

There was a kind of dark medicine chest also, very simply decorated, trimmed with varnished wood and graceless spirals. What did the woman keep in there? The priest stopped to examine everything just so he would not have to look at the woman, with her eyes of harsh fever and sin.

"Have you come, *padre*?" asked the epileptic, even though she could see him right there in the middle of the room with his eyes like altar lamps.

The priest was silent and tried to turn and run away but an extraordinary, violent force seized hold of him, pushing him to take one step forward.

"Come closer!" she said softly. "Have pity! I'm very weak."

He knew everything. He knew that that faint voice was a lie, but at the same time something was hurling him with impunity into the precipice. He was blind; he understood nothing but the raging blood charging through his brains.

He went closer, blindly, his hand outstretched, groping in the air.

He was not praying, nor was he resisting.

The woman took his hand in hers, whereupon the priest felt her warm flesh in the very marrow of his bones. She was indeed feverish and her fever was piercing, as if her hands were a more essential part of her body and not just extremities, something essential and already consummated.

'Sit down, *padre!*"

When the priest heard himself referred to in this way, he felt conscious of the most hideous incest. He was not a *padre*. He was not a father.

"Go away," he would have wanted to plead, but his voice could not be articulated in his throat.

The woman then did something absolutely unheard of. The priest's hand was led under the sheets and placed on her chest, on one of her throbbing breasts.

It was a breast. Nothing else in the world but a burning, solid breast. The priest closed his eyes and squeezed. At first he squeezed intending a repentant caress and then, enraged, impotent, defeated and furious with sin, he dug his nails into her flesh. He felt blood on his fingers but he kept on squeezing.

"You're crazy!" the woman shouted, jumping out of bed half-naked.

The priest stumbled, drunk and destroyed. He walked around the room and suddenly fled into the street.

It began to rain deafeningly and the large drops fell on his face, pounding his forehead. It was an unexpected and ominous rain, as if the sky wanted to contribute its own testimony. He walked aimlessly along the narrow streets and as he made great efforts to calm his heart, a repeated rage was being born in him again, reminding him that he had not consummated his sin. He tried to think about that picture of the Virgin, the wooden medicine chest, the brass bed, anything. It was a dirty, ugly, and extremely high bed—when the priest sat on it his feet did not reach the floor—and it was stained and almost completely chipped. And, once again the demon woman looked strange and seductive lying there on the high bed between the slow blankets that emitted the murmuring of down and sweat.

"You're getting wet, *padre*," he heard a humble voice.

He turned around and there under a door frame was Eduarda, timid, her eyes indulgent and pure.

Eduarda was the only prostitute in the village. Young field workers would visit her, receiving their sexual baptism with fear and somewhat timidly, returning to their shacks with self-confidence and a deeper voice. Now, in the corner protecting herself from the rain, she appeared strange, unique, a seductress of male virgins, with something very transparent, clear, clean, and immaculate about her.

The priest opened his eyes in terror. The mere sound of a female voice usually weakened his spirit, but on this occasion—and this was what surprised him—it appeared to be a new call, an invitation to something unknown.

Eduarda moved as if guilty and repentant when she saw the priest's face which she judged to be choleric. It had been difficult for her to address him since she did not consider herself worthy of that right. How was a prostitute to address a priest?

"Excuse me, *padre*."

The priest's face, with suddenly very painful features, had lost its composure to such a degree that the prostitute felt a deep compassion.

"Come in," she dared to say. "Don't get wet. I'll wait here outside so as not to tempt you."

The priest had never heard anyone talk to him in such a direct, simple, and precise way. "So as not to tempt you." Pronounced like one immense word, bestowing him a dignity and a freedom he had lacked until then. For in recognizing herself as an object of temptation, the prostitute had bestowed upon the priest a powerful and new gift. Once again it made him a chaste being, trustworthy and free.

He entered Eduarda's house while the woman remained motionless by the door, under the rain.

It was dark inside, with a slight odor of clothing, not a dirty odor, just the smell of human clothing filled with a living body. "In this room," he said to himself, "Eduarda gives herself." But to the contrary of what might have been expected, he had thought up this sentence considering the fact attentively and with great independence and clarity, without being blinded with desire. He took a chair and humbly sat down with his arms crossed, his mind resting in silence.

He heard a voice in the street:

"Will you let me in?" It was a man's voice, shaded with base cynicism.

And Eduarda:

"I can't now."

A curse, then the man went away with strong steps which suddenly seemed innocent. Eduarda remained alone, tangible under the rain. But the priest was unexpectedly startled. Had that really happened? That voice? Because everything was a barbarous quietude where things were becoming unraveled, and it was not known whether the rain, the woman, or the door were really happening and were something alive. "Where am I?" he asked himself. "What am I going to do?"

"Eduarda!" he called softly, "Eduarda!"

First, there was a sound; the extraterrestrial, profound sound of the door opening so the woman could come in with her body occupying the Universe. She said something that the priest had forgotten today, but it was something like, "I've come back, I'm here for you," since she had been traveling the earth for two hundred years like an immaterial saint, celestial, ancient, young, full, and fruitful.

Such was his memory.

The water had risen above the priest's shoulders. Now it was going to rise up to his lips and penetrate his mouth with inexorable fury. But he remained on his knees, waiting for death.

His thighs and torso had already turned into stone, like a column. A kind of numbness was rising through his body finally losing him. He had already died in more than half of his body, and soon his sterile heart would become frozen, oxidized, inside the wall of stone.

He then remembered the days of war when the village had armed itself, full of hate.

At that time there were many men, women, and peasants in his church, their hopeless expressions falling like lead.

"They want to crucify Jesus again," said the priest, and a frigid and hopeless deafness responded to his words.

These are the words that would later become blood and fire and weeping. When they are first formed, they are nothing, just a small, unconscious pulmonary force; but when they enter a man they become hardened and demand tribute.

The men took to the mountains, and the priest hid in order to officiate secretly at night.

Everything was dirty and sordid. Their faces had lost their devotion and profundity. He looked at them, in those houses where he said mass, and he saw how they had a lustful, dishonest air about them. The old women would kiss his hand, bestowing upon him the illegitimate dignity of an armed leader, a bloody leader, while the peasants died.

Someone told him the story of a man: the *federales* had taken him prisoner in the morning. He was a poor peasant whom no one knew; he was barefoot, not even wearing *huaraches*. He had a humble, frayed little serape he did not want to part with. He did nothing when the *federales* finally apprehended him.

"It's all right, *mis jefes*," he whispered with resignation when he found out they were going to kill him.

"What else can I do?" he thought. "My turn has come!"

He folded his serape and put it on his shoulder, making him look humble and gentle. It was a handwoven serape of uncarded wool, but he considered it an infinite refuge.

What would he do without it?

Sometimes these poor, brown peasant faces do say something. They say something in spite of their furtive looks and rigid, motionless muscles. The man had something like a smile on his face: but no, it was only a barely perceptible grimace when he had realized he was going to die.

"What's your name?" asked the official.

The peasant did not take his eyes off the ground.

"What's this for, *señor*? Kill me and get it over with."

He was singing as he said this, grief-stricken, his voice breaking, his chin on his chest.

"And why are you a *Cristero*?" the official continued almost teasingly.

"Because of what must be, *señor*," replied the Indian with his previous broken, tearful, and melodic tone, "since they want to kill *Diosito*, our little God.'

The beloved baked clay *Diosito* who was like his coarse and primitive woolen serape. He had undoubtedly seen him somewhere or other, and he would weep inconsolably or drink alcohol until he died if they harmed *Diosito*.

"Fine, that's all well and good. But what's your name?"

The peasant took off his hat and held it in his hands as a sign of respect and humility, and looking at his feet he insisted:

"I already told you, *jefe*, kill me and get it over with."

It was his form of silent, slithering, and tenacious rebellion.

"*Hombre*!" the official continued, "it's just so I can complete the report."

The peasant lowered his head even more, no longer responding.

"We'll call you Juan Perez then."

And immediately addressing the soldiers:

"Get going, *muchachos*!" he ordered cheerfully.

The pair of impassive, brown soldiers were exactly the same as the peasant. They pushed him with the butts of their rifles, with cruel gentleness, leading him to a nearby cork oak tree. The robust, self-assured official followed the group.

The official mounted one of the three horses while the two soldiers tied the peasant's hands behind him. When they were finished they mounted the remaining two horses while Juan Pérez, tied up next to them, waited with his eyes lost and his mind fixed on who knows what.

The air was full of earth and sun. The three horsemen took up their march, and then Juan Pérez's serape, since he had no hands to hold it, slid off and fell to the ground. Juan

Pérez turned his head to look at his little serape, understanding how hopeless his situation was.

The official's horse was young and handsome. It immediately began to run, excited by the air and the rough, pungent morning. Both soldiers galloped after him while Juan Pérez ran behind them with all his soul, hatless, heaving violently, his eyes wide open.

Finally the group stopped under an enormous tree. They dismounted and pushed Juan Pérez under a branch. The peasant's lips and face were ashen.

"Make the knot," said one of the soldiers to his companion, handing him the fine rope of wild lettuce.

Juan Pérez no longer existed for any of the three men. He was simply a strange, wretched being, an animal who spoke but obviously did not suffer. They placed the noose around his neck while he observed everything as if it all had no effect on him whatsoever.

"*Viva Cristo Rey*! Long live Christ the King," he shouted with eyes like steel and his lips pressed tightly together.

No one paid any attention to him.

He jerked up through the air kicking, his body exhausted and distorted.

"Lower him, let him rest!" ordered the official.

"*Viva Cristo Rey!*" was Juan Pérez's reply.

"Raise him again, so he'll stop shouting," said the official, cold and without emotion.

Two, three, four times, and always his stubborn and grim "*Viva Cristo Rey!*" because it was not Christ but rather something terrible, immortal, and nameless that pounded next to his heart and that did not stop pounding even after his heart was in the air, dead inside the body, swaying slightly in the breeze.

The priest remembered this story but he could no longer

remember anything else. Not even the hideous crimes of the *Cristero* soldiers themselves.

The stone was approaching his heart and his body was dying. A burst of wind made him swallow a large quantity of water.

He needed to shout an expiatory word, the same word he had earlier intended to shout to Ursulo and his friends.

"Adán!" he had planned to say.

But he leaned back gently and disappeared into the water.

VII

It was so pale, barely a patch of light, it could have been the moon. The sickly sun suddenly appeared at the zenith, its power softened by the gray clouds; it was a nocturnal, ghostly sun.

The downpour had ceased and a cold rain was the only thing left above that shapeless immensity, which could not possibly be countryside or village or land or human habitat. An incurable sun, a specter at best, like a blind eye rocking from right to left in the stormy sky. The rain was hurling its vertical rays straight down. However, it was not rain but rather a cloak of repeated words. A widowed eye to contemplate solitude and martyrdom, which like a feverish bell was silently banging against the black, green, gray, and grim wool of the clouds.

They must have already died and this was probably what followed life: clouds, bells, and the eye of a cyclops in the middle of the Universe, perhaps even God.

They were actually walking inside their own coffins and their living flesh had turned into crackling, funereal wood.

Everyone—Ursulo, Marcela, Calixto, and Cecilia—stopped before some kind of obstacle. They had been walking without any kind of opposition, almost freely. But suddenly, there it was, something very hard, a condensation of everything and at the same time a perpendicular, dry mass blocking their way. And although they could touch it, it inspired uncertainty in them because how could it now appear here after so much time? And the sun, moving from side to side, a celestial stallion.

As if the air suddenly had doors or walls or boundaries.

Yes, the terrifying sun of another planet, not of the earth, dancing like the sometimes black sun of navigators. Like the sun of shipwreck victims and at the same time like a sinister moon, a yellow, sickly sun of saffron.

The rope was still joining them and they were walking through the water in the twisting, difficult world that existed after death. The priest had disappeared a long time ago and no one seemed unnerved by that fact. They were convinced from the very beginning that when they least expected it they would be disappearing one by one.

Everyone was dead and Ursulo, the deadest of all, was pressing Cecilia's hand in his; and Calixto's hand was in Cecilia's, and the final hand was Marcela's in Calixto's, forming the chain.

What could that obstacle be that was blocking their way as if the falling rain had become sheets of metal or stone? Ursulo opened his eyes wide: the obstacle was his house, around which they had been circling nonstop during those infinite years. Therefore, everything, Jerónimo's death, the priest's disappearance, Calixto's love for Cecilia, had unraveled right there, without their having gone far from their starting point.

They did not move from where they stood and they no longer felt any anguish or grief. They were dead, they felt dead, and sensed it would be useless to go on. An enormous, intense silence followed. It was terrifying to see how the water was flowing without the slightest sound, rising in a silent, stonelike dream. The merciless water was a thinking being of monstrous consciousness. If they did not die they would kill themselves, reflecting the extent to which death had already become an idea in their souls. They desired it and went toward it with fatal, sure steps; they simply wanted solemnity, an internal solemnity that would give them time to welcome death intimately and lovingly to the inexorable house of the body. Death was entering without causing fear, and never would there be heard a shout or lament from them while it slithered through the rooms of resignation.

"We've got to go up to the roof," said Ursulo.

And, without knowing why, everyone climbed up: Calixto, Cecilia, Marcela.

Ursulo held up Chonita's body.

"Take her!"

She existed, she was burning, present, and dead.

Now that he was once again giving up his daughter, if only for a few instants, Ursulo doubted: "Would it not be better for him to go away and become lost?" He would go away and give up his place, leaving Calixto and Cecilia on the roof with Marcela. But this was only a sudden thought. Repentant, he also climbed up to the roof and, facing Cecilia once again, his heart was seized by a sense of affirmation. There before him was his wife. If he had proposed it, if he had given an order to that submissive she-beast, he could have possessed her right there, in spite of the unusual circumstances, right there before Calixto's and Marcela's eyes. If he had proposed it. He nevertheless understood that such a proposal was not possible, because Cecilia was no longer his. "How to get close to her again, to become part of her body once more?"

"My Cecilia," he whispered against his will.

Cecilia's eyes were cold and it would have been better not to have summoned them; they settled on Ursulo without expression and without really looking at him. Ursulo then felt himself to be suddenly left on this earth alone and hopelessly defeated.

Their bodies were coffins of ordinary wood, dead trees, absolutely incapable of blossoming. A strange grave-digger was leading them through the world followed by the deaf multitude. Cecilia, already faceless and nameless. Ursulo was remembering Cecilia's protruding jaws, her large, brown eyes, her chiselled cheekbones, and the birds that lighted on her enormous mouth. Her sex was like a wound, and this thought, although up until then unformulated, nevertheless had always made Ursulo uneasy. There was a certain resistance, a certain repugnance in her to allow herself to be possessed by Ursulo, as if her wound, her bloody sex, must never be touched. Then Ursulo thought about "the other man," Natividad, because he could not get Cecilia's first love and profound surrender off his mind.

Not today. Cecilia without features, without a face, was simply like a smooth surface, the rear-view of a head with no hair, without lips, without a nose.

Even right up to the moment Chonita died, Cecilia's forehead had usually revealed the transparency of her material, three-dimensional ideas, ideas that took up time and space. Today her forehead revealed no shadows, as if she had really died. Who was this woman, this heavy, unfeminine body from the world beyond this one?

They were all lying in their respective coffins, caskets with legs, confined to the naked roof. The procession was infinite, and the air was giving birth to voices and looks that dragged along.

Cecilia's body had been delicate and smooth. And it had died so suddenly at Chonita's death!

When Chonita's sickness began, a feverish glow appeared in her mother's eyes. Cecilia obviously did not want her to die, but something monstrous, a demon, was entering her soul. Her daughter's sickness was permitting her a small triumph over Ursulo. Perhaps this is bestial but it happens and it happened to Ursulo and Cecilia.

That child vomited blood the first time. She was a flower with rotting roots, fading daily, almost totally bloodless. Her eyes had grown and her arms had become so large they had already reached the height of the doorknob. She had not really begun to talk yet—she was all of 10 or 15 months old— but in her death agony she actually said so many things in her heavy breathing that the air in the room became thick and yellow. She was going to die, and both of them, Ursulo and Cecilia, had understood this from the very first moment. A frozen fever was penetrating her through her fingernails which were the first to die, with their slight color of purple corn. They were kernels of corn growing through her fingers, as inside a deadly earth, and they rose up with ears, with their leaves of early, atrocious autumn.

"Chonita is going to die," said Cecilia.

She loved her daughter deeply, which was precisely why it was shattering and terrifying to discover that deep down and against her will she was hoping that Chonita would die. Ursulo's presence in Chonita could not be denied, and it was enraging and maddening that while they lived Chonita had been the reference point for both of them, their place of meeting.

Ursulo had not impregnated Cecilia because of any impulse to procreate but rather simply to possess her totally, to take possession of her soul. This rare proprietor did not seek the body but rather the dominion of the spirit, and he had raped Cecilia's most inalienable parts.

"Do you understand? Chonita is going to die," she repeated.

Ursulo looked at her with a humble wretched stare.

"Yes," he said sadly.

He was about to lose his great, stubborn love. With a sense of fatality, he then decided not to do anything to save Chonita. Let everything be consummated and let the tragic destiny of solitude arrive.

The nights had been endless beside the opaque oil lamp. From the first day the child began to breathe with shadows in her throat, and perhaps her lungs were like a dark bag in which the air moved blindly, tripping on the sharp angles of death.

Cecilia and Ursulo had not said a word to each other, both of them absorbed by that criminal presence. Cecilia was moaning as she applied alcohol, iodine, and other fragrances that penetrated through pores. A bell of smoked glass was swinging in the room and inside an enormous, disoriented fly was buzzing with its gray wings.

Something like a small light, and like a plaster mask without features, was at the window. Ursulo noticed its exact presence. He got up to open the door and see, but no, there was no one outside. He did this three or four times, and each time he found that emptiness next to the window; but inside, through the distorting window pane, there it was: obstinate, infinite, cold, but also sweet, sad, compassionate, the face.

"Why do you keep going out?" asked Cecilia.

Ursulo was unable to answer her, but he must have stared at her so absurdly and so totally because suddenly they both hopelessly understood. Death was at the window. Then it entered the room and there in the chair it waited for the instant it would have to lean over the little body under the mosquito netting.

Now Chonita was on the roof, blurred, insignificant, a tiny bundle, with signs of worms underneath her concave blood. On the river bank, next to Marcela, she was a paper boat, pink *papier de Chine*, looking as if about to set sail. But the sad truth was that the tiny paper boat would never set sail, with the odor of water that turned green as it fell over the moss that was already covering everything.

Calixto's eyes remained riveted to the corpse. He was staring in a stupefied way from which there was emerging, nevertheless, a certain special intelligence directed at one single object, as if his brain had suddenly acquired the capacity to understand one single but important and profound revelation. That corpse was also his, as much his as it was Ursulo's. Because if there were one thing that had brought them together there it was Chonita; but it was a dead Chonita, and she was already beginning to rot.

Calixto recalled that Chonita's birth had not really produced the slightest impression among them. On the other hand, the knowledge that Cecilia was pregnant really had. Chonita's birth had simply served as an excuse to get drunk until dawn. They preferred the corpse, they were more interested in death itself, and, ugly and gaunt, they had all attended the wake in order to pay their respects and remember, surrendering to a secret nostalgia.

Ursulo had noticed Calixto intensely staring at the corpse.

"What are you looking at?" he shouted brutally and unintentionally, unable to contain himself, clenching his fists.

The idea that another man, other men, were attempting to take legal possession of this corpse that properly and intimately belonged only to him enraged him. It belonged to him for all of the reasons in the world: for his love for Cecilia, for the drama of his solitary, hungry life, for his origins, and for death, at whose frontier he now found himself.

Calixto, totally oblivious to Ursulo's shout, continued staring at Chonita: there it was, that immaculate and mysterious understanding, his negation and his freedom: because in some dark way, he, Calixto, had penetrated Cecilia's life, through her dead daughter, and today he was a father looking down on that small, cold body, immediately establishing a relationship between him and his desired, beloved woman through pain, solitude, and the uncontainable fury of finding himself lost and abandoned. He got up slowly, as if in a dream, and headed toward the little *papier de Chine* boat. He pressed it into his arms wrapping himself up in the clouds and fog that were being born there like a gloomy dawn.

"Leave her alone!" Ursulo ordered with rage.

Calixto, drunk and only partially awake, opened his eyes, totally unable to understand what Ursulo was trying to say.

Chonita had not mattered in life. She mattered now that she was simply a link to the beyond, profoundly uniting their destinies.

She was born in the afternoon, a little before sunset: the air becomes thin right before the sun dies, and a few black birds, like stones, silently cross the air, as if fleeing some danger.

On the horizon the clouds were aflame, suggesting that an inconceivable frontier was beginning at the end of which would be an infinite valley of gold. Nevertheless, the illusion scattered as soon as the sun sank below the horizon, and the clouds, which had earlier been clear and luminous, began with their violet, deep purple color, until becoming gray like embers.

Ursulo's friends were sitting on the bench in front of one of the Irrigation System's wooden houses. Ursulo arrived and was cautious.

"It was a girl," he told them, trying not to show any emotion.

He then proposed that they go and drink. Drink all of whatever there was. They headed for the bar, *La Negra Consentida*.

"What day is it today?" Ursulo asked the bartender.

The bartender assumed the gesture of an uncertain fortune-teller.

"Maybe Friday?"

Ursulo smiled.

"No, I don't mean that. I wanted to know what saint we celebrate today."

The bartender examined the dirty, faded calendar, announcing a large grocery store with its photo of an elegant, colorful, smiling peasant girl, riding sidesaddle on a handsome steed.

"The Incarnation of the Lord. That's it, today is The Incarnation."

Ursulo smiled again.

"What do you think?"

They served several large, transparent glasses of tequila.

"The Incarnation. So we'll call her Chona, Chonita."

In an hour and a half everyone was completely drunk. Ursulo, leaning on Calixto's shoulder, mumbled gloomily:

"It's really a pity that the late Natividad could not be here. I'd have made him my *compadre*, by God."

The relationship between Ursulo and Natividad had been curious. More precisely, the relationship that existed from Ursulo toward Natividad.

Natividad arrived at the Irrigation System and a short time later all the farm laborers had risen to declare a general strike. Ursulo had been opposed to the strike at the beginning, because he correctly saw himself affected as a landholder. However, one conversation with Natividad was enough to convince him. Natividad told him that he was the miserable landholder of only fifteen *hectares*, and that the strike was actually against the large landholders. Ursulo joined the movement accompanied by his two laborers.

Natividad captivated Ursulo; he wished he could be like him: honest, strong, militant, loyal. Especially because Cecilia admired and loved him. When Natividad succeeded in winning Cecilia's love, instead of this fact instilling hatred in him, it served unexpectedly to make Ursulo feel doubly attracted to this man. When Natividad was murdered, Ursulo nevertheless experienced very diverse and contradictory emotions: a certain unconfessed satisfaction, of course, and a rage, a desire to emulate Natividad and realize his goals, his ideas, even accepting the ultimate consequences no matter how crazy and absurd they might be. In this way, when the strike failed, Ursulo committed himself to continue on his own. He took root to the land; everyone was leaving and he remained behind, until today, until death.

No, Chonita did not matter in life. What meaning could the fact of someone's appearance in existence have if just the opposite, disappearance, was what truly mattered, when the fatal condition of man is renewed?

It was different when the child died.

It had been raining incessantly for two days and the sky was dark and thick while the filthy river rushed dizzily. It was a treacherous and perverse river, its source unpredictable, dry for most of the year and sometimes even longer, then filling suddenly and erupting furiously inside the fragile bed. The inhabitants of the region lived in submission to the river as if to a blind, whimsical goddess, awaiting either happiness or punishment from its fickleness. Two days and nights, as if the sky were an oppressive, bottomless water tank. What was strange, what intimidated the spirit, was the total lack of light in everything, the blindness and that tenacious roar and chest-pounding over their heads. Something, as if an insane bird were trapped inside, was stirring the apprehensive heart, and the air had become harsher and the rain like a curse.

Calixto was sleeping beside his insomniac wife, who was keeping watch, her eyes full of terror.

It was a hallucination without doubt, because La Calixta felt that everything happening outside, the roar of the wind, the rain, the river, was actually happening inside her, as if she were the earth itself. Her feet, for example, were like two blue mountains along whose slopes the immense water was cascading; but at the same time they were two anguished pyramids pointing up at a wet and spongy sky. The water was digging like fiery volcanic lava into her living flesh. An enormous planet, her stomach was growing larger, and she resembled a choleric bullfrog in the middle of the storm. A storm of broken veins, trees, and an inhuman, savage river was raining down on La Calixta, paralyzing her body and, like an internal sea with its voices and its silent murmur, so too was her very physical being apprehensive and terror-stricken beside her husband who was so far away in the depths of sleep.

A voice sounded inside her as if from a grave.

"Calixta, Calixta!"

Yes, the voice was inside her, faint, making its way through an organic and resistant jungle.

"Calixta!"

But no. The voice was coming from outside, soaked and trembling.

"Open the door, please!"

Clumsily, La Calixta got up to light a candle. Yes, this voice was the voice of someone else, it was that velvety and unreal voice she was hearing in her abdomen.

When she opened the door, there was Cecilia, silent, with her large, nocturnal eyes. Chonita had died.

She was already dead, with her pink dress and she grieved for not having seen her surrender her soul.

They had surrounded her when they saw her lying on top of the soap crates in Ursulo's house as if she were alive. Then a wind began to blow and the candles were flickering, hollow, distant, long, and surrounded with darkness.

Today, in Calixto's arms, Chonita resembled a small paper boat.

Enraged, Ursulo grabbed Calixto by the shirt and shouted again:

"I told you to let her go!"

That corpse mattered.

Cecilia was contemplating the scene with indifference, while Marcela, who had grown pale, tried to stop the two men from fighting.

But it was too late. Ursulo threw a punch and the blow knocked them both off the roof. They continued fighting in the water for another instant, until finally, perhaps because of exhaustion, perhaps not, the clash ended, and with great difficulty both men climbed back up, Ursulo lovingly pressing Chonita's drenched, abused body to his own.

No one said a word. A silence engulfed everything, while Ursulo and Calixto, their heads bowed, began to sink into a mortal and final sadness.

VIII

They had already spent three days on the roof and were so weak they were unable to utter a single word; they were near death, breathing with difficulty.

Life finally surrenders and an indefinable feeling of anxious resignation impels one to look at everything with careful, fervent eyes, and things begin to take on their humanity and a warmth of steps, inhabited footprints. The world is not alone; rather, man dwells on it. Its vastness, and all the land it covers, the stars, animals, trees, it all makes sense. We should stop one of these clear nights and look up toward the sky: that constellation, that solitary planet, all this symphonic material that vibrates in an ordered, rigorous way, would it have any meaning were it not for eyes to see it, eyes, simply animal or human eyes, from any point in the universe, from here or from Uranus? Life finally surrenders and a hope, a secret exultation utters words, universal notions: the situation today, death, an eternity. I exist and this fact is communicated to me by my body and my spirit, both of which are about to cease to exist; I have participated in the unspeakable miracle, I have belonged. I was a part and a factor, and life has given me an immaculate dignity, similar to what stars, seas, or clouds might have. Although I am late in realizing this, this minute in which it has been revealed to me is the greatest and most solemn of my life. I lean my head on my chest; my heart is the purest of flags.

From up above, a flock of *zopilotes* was circling stubbornly, the buzzards drawn by the scent of Chonita's decaying carcass. Those *zopilotes* would descend fatally, vile vultures waiting for man's powerlessness even before the shipwreck victims had died. So, lacking in energy to fight back, these totally abandoned human creatures would have to permit their insides to be slowly devoured. Prometheans lost.

The group formed by Cecilia, Ursulo, Calixto, and Marcela was a heroic, courageous group with its corpse: Cecilia emaciated, wretched, wrinkled, wounded, and nearly insane, her lips gray; Calixto persevering, surviving; Marcela calm, like a collective mother; Ursulo in defeat.

Calixto was clearly the strongest of the group. He had arrived in the region a few years earlier, immediately after the Irrigation System had been inaugurated. Calixto was tall, with narrow shoulders and a thin face. He was harsh, crude, with large, hairy hands. His eyes had something peculiar and unpleasant about them; they stared out deep-set and dead, as if they were false eyes, glass eyes, solid and cloudy.

General Villa finally laid down his arms and went to live on his hacienda which he called Canutillo. At that point the Division of the North was dissolved and discharged; some soldiers went over to join the army and others returned to their homes. Calixto was one of the latter even though he had no home to go to.

The colonel harangued them:

"So, my sons, whoever wants to stay in the army just say so, and whoever doesn't want to let him make it back to his house."

Calixto made it back with the money he had obtained in

the struggle: approximately 10,000 pesos in jewels, and he was only a second lieutenant.

He had not forgotten how he had obtained the jewels.

It had been a cold, impenetrable morning. The horses' hides were quivering nervously and the frozen rifle bolt was hurting his hands. They had had to wrap the horses' hoofs in sacks of straw so they would not make noise, and they produced a silent, reptilian sound, as if they were riding over gigantic lizards. Here and there soldiers were cursing in whispers.

Most amazing and terrifying of all was the surprise attack they had planned for that dawn; open combat is different even though there one is also terrified. And it happens like this: first there is a change in one's voice; it is no longer the same voice, but instead slightly someone else's; one hears it as if it were coming from somewhere else, and it is wondrous and mysterious the way this someone else begins to penetrate one's being, someone unknown and capable of who knows what. One repeats the word: "Fuck!" and it is really another throat, another voice. Then such a special state of unconsciousness occurs in which the critical spirit declares itself free and one can go right up to his own body and watch himself run, demented, cold, rabid, and without hope.

But entering a city secretly in the darkness borders on anguish. One must defend himself from the shadows where there is an enemy breathing, a face that cannot be seen, a man who takes aim with the cold barrel of his rifle, in other words a silent, obstinate legion with unlimited bodies.

On that night something was happening similar to another time when the leader of the column had ordered his men to cross a canyon. It had been a splendid day, clear and peaceful. Intermittently and without rhyme or reason, the soft breeze gently bent the grass so that later everything looked in absolute harmony. But still ahead of them, the two peaks forming the canyon were announcing their enigma: the unexpected, the incomprehensible, the possibility that death was lying there in wait. Could not the enemy remain silent and patient while waiting for the column?

And now, right there between the houses, could not the same thing be true?

The voices in each man were now clearly beginning to sound alien, and a sensation of limpness gave a certain abandon to their bodies, a certain nonexistence to their muddy, impersonal limbs.

When they assaulted the city, they were all seized with an uncertainty and then with a certain haste, a desire for everything to happen once and for all.

Cities have a particular odor, you can tell that they are filled with sleeping bodies and families all of whose pulsations rise into the air.

This city was spread out right there before them, black like a more clearly defined dark stain amid the shadows.

Calixto was thinking: "I'll arrive with eight men; if I encounter resistance, we'll break the door down."

He had been there as a small boy, when he was eight or ten years old, but he still remembered the large, somber, and solemn study. But perhaps it had merely been enlarged by the eyes of memory. For example, when he saw the hacienda's patio again he saw a rather small patio with its puny, melancholy tree. But earlier the patio had been as immense as the earth and climbing the tree had been an entire adventure. In the study, a table whose red tablecloth was now faded with age, used to wobble, dancing under the weight of Don Melchor's movements.

Don Melchor had asked him an endless barrage of questions: How old are you? What's your name? Do you know how to read? Who sent you? Do you know how to work? Are you an orphan? Are you from around here? Who were your parents? To which Calixto had responded as best he could. Later he was sent to the hacienda as a child laborer. And at that time the patio had seemed enormous.

The somber study revealed its solid, antique furniture, which appeared to have intensified or increased its gravitational pull, attaching itself to the floor with fierce determination as if with monstrous roots: tall chairs as if for priests or solemn prelates stood next to the rusty bookcase.

Hanging from the ceiling, a crystal chandelier seemed to be moving, albeit imperceptibly. It was huge and majestic, but it looked as if it were actually swinging a millimeter back and forth. Calixto's flustered eyes were staring at it in order to surprise it in the act of moving, while he was shrinking, fearing it would crash down on him. Was it an illusion? Staring, he suddenly saw that it was true. It was moving slightly, slowly.

"What are you looking at so hard?" Don Melchor's shout woke him.

Confused, Calixto lowered his head, but he continued thinking that the chandelier was definitely going to swing and all of a sudden fall and smash them mercilessly.

There was also a painting on the wall with its *señora* posing in it, her still living eyes shining between her cheekbones, giving the study the tone and atmosphere of an immense broken music box. She was a *señora* with a black velvet ribbon around her neck and in her diminutive hands painted so small to flatter her she held a holy book with metal clasps. The study was like a music box, because it resembled a broken-down jewel and at the same time because a certain grace had simply lingered unnoticeably in the room.

During the cross-examination a man came in whose glasses shone insolently when he looked at Calixto. He leaned over with great ceremony and placed some papers on the table. Don Melchor stood straight up, equally ceremoniously:

"*Señor licenciado!*"

If the chandelier were to break loose it would fall exactly on top of the *Señor licenciado*. Calixto retreated to one side of the room near the priestly chairs from where he could see a dreamlike spectacle of splendor: Don Melchor, his back to the visitor, opened the large cabinet and took out a bag filled with coins. Then, throughout the entire room, like a resurrection, as if everything old or dusty had become young, strong, and hopeful, a ringing of little bells was heard coming from the gold coins.

This was an unforgettable moment, and, now that it was a question of pillaging the city, Calixto was again imagining the sound of those little bells.

He would go to the house with eight of his men and open the solemn, venerable door carved with savage, masculine roughness.

They were a few steps from the village. In the darkness a first captain approached Calixto:

"We have arrived," he said with a calm, gloomy voice. "You go in with your men over there on that side. Go in firing into the air but shoot on the spot anyone you see."

A terror, a silent question, could be felt everywhere. There is always something that you cannot predict, like the neighing of a horse which could ruin everything. There are a thousand such details about which one must think with uneasiness and anxiety.

Villa's troops entered the city shooting right and left.

It was a dark city. The random bullets made different sounds: sometimes a whistle, or a hollow detonation, and there was always the small lightless flash.

It was a nocturnal jungle, with insomniac birds that chirp and flutter. The horses, disabled centaurs, were stirring with fear before the enigma, pulling back.

Then there were the tiny lights of cigarettes:

"Don't smoke, we'll be sitting targets!"

A soothing, supernatural smoke, that mattered as much as a woman or life itself.

Perhaps someone from the other side had fallen during the shooting. But where was that other side?

Calixto's voice sounded hoarse; he was frightened and his face was pale:

"Here it is!"

The horses' haunches looked like the most rounded part of the darkness, moving and human, bunched together in front of the door.

Calixto and his men dismounted.

"Yes, here it is!"

The same door carved with roughness, with eternity.

Calixto felt both sides of the twin tritons, with their strong faces, furious eyes, and majestic nobleness.

"Open up!" he banged on the door.

But his men, with unexpected diligence, had already found a wooden beam which they were ready to use as a battering ram.

"Open up in the name of the Revolution!"

They knocked down the door with a loud commotion and fired several perfunctory shots into the air, breaking the silence weighing so heavily on them, tirelessly releasing shouts, yells, and curses as if they could finally breathe.

"Hey, you, bring me a light!"

The torch illuminated the body of a woman trying to hide near the thick pillar of the arches. As soon as she saw their hard faces and savage jaws she began to wail:

"Don't kill me!" raising her hands to her chest.

She was a wretched, terrified old woman. The torch lit an irregular circle around her, illuminating the floor tiles. Further on the large, solitary patio awaited.

"Take me to the *patrón's* study, *abuelita*," said Calixto, almost with tenderness.

As the woman was getting up, looking from side to side, Calixto grabbed her roughly by the breast and thrust his hand into her blouse. Hidden between the old woman's cold, soft breasts, was the purse. Calixto felt the ugly flesh make contact with the palm of his hand, while something absolutely different and coarse, as if covered with sand, was stabbing his fingers. "It's a glass bead purse," he said to himself, but he could not take his mind off the woman's breasts, and he experienced a vivid repugnance at the sudden and unexpected analogy that the breasts he was feeling were those of his mother.

"You old bitch!" he shouted angrily.

The old woman had twenty well-counted gold coins on her.

"Get moving and take me to the *patrón's study!*"

The woman did not say a word. She assumed they would shoot her later. Such was no doubt God's plan, to be shot to death without a prayer, in total darkness. A thousand dizzying memories were boiling in her mind, but what was happening right there in front of her was moving slowly and seemed as if it would never end.

"Stay here!" Calixto ordered his men after dividing the coins among them.

The old woman, followed by Calixto, staggered toward the study.

No, the study was no longer quite so large and even the crystal chandelier seemed less majestic. The portrait of the *señora* with her strange eyes was still hanging on the wall right over the cupboard. She was probably Don Melchor's grandmother or mother, who knows. She was fat, placid, and evil. Her double-chin was barely contained by the velvet ruff, giving her a certain masculine touch. A dull, wistful glow gave her cheeks a slight trace of sensuality and youth, and constituted a certain index of her critical and bitter forty years. But two opposite parts, her hands and her eyes, worked against the ordinary appearance of the montage, and the mere sight of them produced a certain repugnance. If her somewhat spherical bust, chubby shoulders, short snow-white neck and thin forehead were impersonal and typical of the *señoras* of the epoch, her hands, on the contrary, had something unique and unpleasant about them, a lack of generosity. They were deceitful, devout hands, made for the soft, warm baking of chocolates or cookies for the priest. Libidinous, chaste little hands into which the painter, upon transferring them to the canvas, put the only bit of genius he possessed. Her eyes, in turn, were myopic and white, and they completed the vision, calculating eyes with their eyelids and dark circles. Even though the railing or pulpit—in any case something sacred— that served as the background to the figure had actually been painted in order to bestow dignity and devotion upon her, the eyes responded with a veiled audacity, in quite successful counterpoint to all the rest.

Calixto could not resist stopping to look at the portrait which was now generating thoughts so different from those of the first time. It was not fear now, nor that sensation of distance and antiquity; today something mysterious had occurred, as if the power and grandeur that long ago had emanated from the portrait had now been translated to him. A smile formed on his face.

"The hell with it!" he thought.

A certain unexpected rage was grimly taking control of him. He suddenly knew himself to be a free man, powerful and master of his life. He had been so submissive before that the discovery of this new capacity or condition produced in him a strange mixture of joy and hatred. He climbed up onto the cupboard to take down the portrait.

The woman, Don Melchor's wife, grandmother, mother, or aunt, glared with rage at Calixto from those painted eyes so close he could touch them. She was suddenly coming back to life, irascible and alive, with her small hateful hands. The nineteenth-century bust seemed to shake with indignation.

Calixto took out his red handkerchief and meticulously cleaned the painting. Afterward, with his knife, he slit the woman's plump, white throat.

The elderly servant just stood there whimpering, looking at the portrait, her eyes filled with compassion.

"Get out of here!" shouted Calixto.

Calixto could have done anything he pleased in that instant and his blood was racing uncontrollably. He smashed the cupboard door with one blow. His hands were trembling as he touched the small ebony box. There were two crossed swords on the top of the lid. Two swords that could be recognized by touch since Calixto was now blind, walking blindly in a world he directly controlled, but a world surrounded by the abyss.

He had never seen so many jewels at once as when he opened the box: a small mountain of colors poured onto the table. Twenty or twenty-five gold *azteca* coins scattered their fine powder as they fell onto the table.

Calixto's heart was beating irregularly, sometimes feverishly and then suddenly with an anguished slowness. Flee. Escape. He had to get away immediately. Let the revolution come to an end and let a new order be established, with no more revolutions, no more anxiety, no more ambushes. He needed silence, a soothing silence; he needed silence just as one needs water. And why was his heart beating irregularly as if he were suddenly dizzy and then almost stopping as if he were sleepwalking? Security, support, protection. Let them allow him to make off with the jewels and gold and hide in some sheltered place, because otherwise the very next day the filthy, pitiful legion would be asking him for help as if he had a fortune in his hands.

Hatred seized his soul. He hated those who thanks to this miracle of jewels were no longer his equals: the barefoot, the naked. Let them die; let them disappear.

He touched his forehead bathed in sweat and a darkness appeared before his eyes. He was weak and fragile, like a bush deformed by the rain. He leaned on the table so as not to fall, but a dark, rough hand intervened, taking a jewel into its fingers.

Calixto turned, his face filled with terror. One of his men had come in undetected, his enormous *sombrero* on the back of his head and his face innocent, flabbergasted, and smiling. There was no malice in the man. In fact, the jewel filled him with wonder, as if it were simply a prodigious toy, and he laughed showing his large, beautiful peasant teeth.

For some reason, Calixto looked down at the man's feet. He was wearing *huaraches*, and they looked pathetic, extremely humble and deformed, tied to the earth.

Calixto grabbed his pistol.

The man continued smiling.

"Hey, *jefe*," he said, incredulous. "You're not going to kill me?"

He was barely able to finish the sentence because Calixto, already a blind man, fired.

Even after he had died, the man's face still conserved that expression of surprise and disbelief, of finding out that he had gotten himself mixed up in an innocent joke.

Terrifying months were to follow that day, and Calixto fell ill with the delirium of one who is pursued. He would fall asleep with the jewels beside him, his hand on his revolver.

He was searching for the right moment to desert when by happy coincidence they announced the general discharge of the Division of the North.

"The revolution is over," said the colonel. "Now every man can return to his home with what he has earned, or he can write to the secretary of war for them to recognize him and for him to continue in the army. *Viva* my general Francisco Villa!"

"*Vivaaa!*" responded the mass of soldiers.

They found themselves confused. It seemed so difficult to believe that everything had come to an end! What should they do now? Ten years of chaos, disorder, and licentiousness do not transpire in vain. They had wanted everything to go on as always, to go back to the mountains and plains, and the shots, the fear, and the crude and terrifying sensuality of death. A grandiose and inalienable power like an abyss had been revealed to them during the fighting. It was a tempting and primitive power which was soon in their blood, flowing with its venom. They had lost it during the dark days of the persecution and peace of the *Porfiriato* so as to win it back today in the bloody struggle. Only gods were in possession of it since it was the divine and demonic power that took away life, and if the ancestors used to practice it with such solemnity and devotion it was precisely because they aspired to share the attributes of divinity. The gun, therefore, that mechanical and intelligent power so similar to sex, had been incorporated into their very organisms and hearts. After all of this, now that they were capable of killing, it had become impossible for them to consider themselves inferior. It was a power like a sex that ejaculated death. Something mysterious and unknown existed, near or far away, now, today, or tomorrow, or within a few years, and it was subdued by that power of which they were the masters. They could kill.

But how and why was the revolution ending?

The unchallenged colonel, standing right there, was repeating:

"Whoever wants to go home . . . "

110

The *soldaderas* actually did show some curiosity and interest in the new possibilities. They listened to the colonel's words with obvious respect.

The majority of Pancho Villa's unit decided to stay in the army. Only one tall, strong soldier broke loose from the ranks:

"Colonel, sir," he said, "I'd like to work a small piece of land, but where can I find one?"

The colonel seemed surprised:

"Damn! I hadn't thought about that. But grab whatever piece you find and see what happens."

The *soldaderas* and camp followers whispered among themselves, forming a separate group apart, with their baskets and *rebozos*. They were interested in the problem. They would have preferred that all their men went to work the land. But their own land, even though it might be grabbed and taken from wherever.

"And then what do I do if they protest?"

The colonel shrugged his shoulders.

"What do you mean? What do you think you have that rifle for?"

The ranks of warriors celebrated the matter with strident hilarity.

Calixto, in the company of five other ex-*Villistas*, took a military train bound for Mexico City.

For the first time in a long period he contemplated his country's landscape, and a strange, tender smile stamped a certain gentleness on his ugly face.

First, the gloomy, desolate landscape of certain parts of San Luis Potosí. Wastelands, as if a nameless earthquake had left its irrevocable mark on them. Did the wide, limitless land of Mexico actually have inhabitants, or was there nothing but solitary land, with its deep, sad surface? Then, there is a peasant alongside the railroad tracks. He does not move, he does not salute or smile, but instead hides under his long blankets so no one will notice him. To what strange world does he belong? What kind of heart does he have? In the small village, gaunt, stubborn, obsessive women offer the traveler a piece of cured beef. They begin asking for about twenty *centavos* per piece but they finally accept five. And all this is happening amid the landscape of a gray land of wretched shacks from which slowly rises the blue smoke of firewood.

Up ahead the mountains are waiting, the pure force of the country, a force that imposes its solemn and bestial mass wherever one's sense of smell is nourished by fragrant sounds and resin. Uninhabited mountains of the coyote, the wild dog, the sluggish, pensive wild boar, the savage jaguar, the deranged dove, and the animal Indian. Along the crags and imperceptible paths the wounded, naked feet of man and those of the stalking serpent mingle on the same road, with the same destiny. Profound Mexico, without a surface because it is so interior, subterranean, and filled with invisible tears!

Next comes the valley, breathing calmly. Its pyramids preside over everything; even when they are at some distance and cannot be seen, they are noticed, they are felt. They had been placed there religiously and therefore the valley is filled with wisdom and the tapping of the chisel on the stone can be heard, as well as the aquatic blood of the idol. The pyramids can be heard walking while lakes rise up full of birds like a horizontal, terrestrial sky. The clear valley is a sleeping idol, the sculpture of a dream. Acolman, Tepexpan, Xometla, where the cactus grows wing-shaped. Here are the pyramids scattering their dust of transparent stone at sundown. They can be heard, and their distant atmosphere, their thick posing in the immaculate grace of the air, emerges in the very depths of one's eyes.

Suddenly the countryside comes to an end and there appears the hubbub of a city full of children with bloated bellies, patios, posts, mud, clotheslines, and beggars.

When Calixto arrived, the station was full of soldiers, bonfires, and brazen revolutionary women who were staring at the travelers.

He got off the train to lodge in a nearby hotel.

This was Mexico City, dusty, with its small buildings, straight streets, gawky taxi drivers in their speeding, crazed Fords!

Gods and centaurs of white foam to the north and south and all the cardinal points of heaven, these majestic clouds preside over the city, sometimes riding to the west in a gladiator cart pulled by steeds which sparkled with gold, sometimes sitting on thick columns of an arbitrary, round temple, next to the volcanoes: the sturdy arm of the Greek discus thrower over the ancient, calcinated lake of Texcoco, next to the dark thigh of the Indian archer by the mountains of Santa Clara. Violent and solid picture-postcard clouds, where filigree ornamentation is not possible, growing vigorously so that once established over Mexico they give it its aerial, suddenly celestial quality.

While mopping the hotel floors, La Calixta observed how the man who would be her husband stumbled into the office.

She continued observing Calixto from that moment on, with careful attention, astonished at his artificial eyes which resembled those on the heads of dissected animals. (When later they came right up to her face, forcing a vague, terrifying coldness to penetrate her, she did not resist the animal force and surrendered herself without a struggle.)

The administrator of the Continental Hotel, with its horrible and narrow claustrophobic rooms, filthy chamber pots, and horrible mirrors, maintained La Calixta as his concubine. He was a man of medium stature, quick, cautious eyes, and vicious conduct. In the evenings, prostitutes worked out of the hotel, and he charged them fifty *centavos* per client as his cut. The strange thing was that the prostitutes actually considered him their benefactor for the simple fact that he did not call the police on them.

La Calixta was beaten daily, and for no reason, by the administrator. He felt he had to beat her because women were basically stupid and could be managed only with beatings. She accepted the beatings submissively, always exaggerating the pain they caused her.

She had observed Calixto that first time, when he had entered the hotel room followed by a man in a black suit. The door was left half open and La Calixta managed to hear part of their conversation.

"It's a good haul," said the stranger's voice.

Their voices suddenly became hushed, and despite her efforts La Calixta was unable to hear them. But then:

"Only in the United States. Here it would be too dangerous."

A strange mystery was unraveling there. The United States! La Calixta had heard talk about this distant, white, golden country. Suddenly the mere mention of the words was like being in a port, standing on the dock of a wharf. The sea, with its wakes, was providing a road and a refuge. Calixto acquired a new meaning in the eyes of the woman. If he wanted, he could free her and take her far away. Very far away, to the United States.

No other words were heard and a little later the second man left the room.

Since the door had remained open, La Calixta approached the threshold. There, with his back to her, Calixto was leaning over the night table. Suddenly, sensing this strange presence, he turned abruptly.

They looked at each other without saying a word, both inexplicably dazed, until La Calixta, driven by an unknown impulse, suddenly broke out in tears telling him of the anguish and suffering she was forced to endure there in the hotel.

"Take me with you," she begged; "I heard that you're going to the United States! I know that you will beat me less." She was only asking for a little less harshness, less brutality, conjecturing that Calixto, at worst, would be more understanding than the others. She therefore begged with great insistence and tears.

Calixto was convinced by that one phrase: "You will beat me less."

La Calixta was not so very mistaken. Her husband attacked her and beat her only from time to time, and particularly when he was drunk.

But she never forgot one savage beating that almost killed her.

On the morning of that day, the man dressed in black who had previously met with Calixto in the Continental Hotel, came to their house as reserved and cautious as always. Calixto and his wife were at that time living in Ciudad Juarez.

As on that first occasion, La Calixta tried to hear everything:

"My client does not want to come," said the voice, for some reason hoarse as if feverish or pressured. "He wants me to bring the jewels to him."

Following these words came a silence during which La Calixta could envision Calixto's scowling, suspicious face.

"No," he said firmly. "That's impossible. Have him come here."

In case the client agreed to deal with him there, Calixto had already thought out all his plans. He would observe the exchange from the other side of the door, because he was in no way willing to be hustled by the jewel fence and his alleged client. Behind the door, with his pistol in his hand, he would burst in at precisely the instant he observed any suspicious sign in order to surprise and punish whoever intended to rob him.

"That's impossible," he repeated.

How could he let the fence take the jewels just like that?

There was a heavy silence.

"All right, don Calixto," responded the fence in an angry tone, "nothing has been lost. Maybe some other time."

The man left the house and La Calixta could see in his face a curious, extremely irate and determined expression.

Calixto had arranged the sale of the jewels and for this reason had moved to the border. It was a delicate operation, where Calixto would only figure in as a shadow, behind the fence.

When he left the capital he took La Calixta with him. He needed a woman.

In reality, La Calixta was not ugly, with her elongated, oval face and her straight black hair. Perhaps before her harsh treatment and suffering had brutalized her, she might have been intelligent and sharp. But now her face was dull and when asked about anything she would meditate slowly and obstinately, unable to answer promptly even when it was about the simplest thing.

Calixto had observed her sharp, not uncomely chin, but what had most attracted him were the signs of her hopelessness: an apprehension, a burning desire for refuge, which made her definitely submissive to any man capable of transmitting to her his force and security.

Beside her, Calixto felt as if fresh, docile, and invigorating waters were being added to the current of his own life.

He went with her to the border, explaining to her in vague terms the purpose of the trip, an unnecessary explanation as it turned out since La Calixta was incapable of any profound curiosity, indolent as she was and so busy with matters of her own self which had become seized by strange anxieties.

The jewel fence was waiting for Calixto in Ciudad Juarez. Small, smiling, clever, and smart, he had made Calixto's acquaintance in Mexico City.

He was a man for whom no epoch of his life had been as splendid as that of the revolution. The revolution was jewels. An entire society enamored of jewels was crumbling and the fantastic stones were breaking free from the edifice: amethysts, rubies, diamonds, pearls. A decrepit, old, conservative, and reactionary regime begins by accumulating jewels, and when the masses finally intervene with a revolution, those jewels gradually begin to appear, passing from hand to hand until they reach those smooth, diligent, friendly, understanding, and cordial hands of men like Calixto's fence.

In Eagle Pass alone, the fence had said, a client was offering 10,000 pesos for Calixto's jewels, but he had to see them.

No. Calixto refused flatly. He was not going to entrust the jewels naïvely to the fence.

"All right, don Calixto," said the fence.

He was a small man, dressed in a dark suit and with immaculate manners.

In the afternoon, Calixto had gone to the tavern and he did not return until very late at night, in a wretched state. He had a deep head wound, and his matted, stiff hair was sticking to his temples, mixing with the blood. Completely covered with mud, he was tottering by the door as if he were going to fall. However, not only did he remain steady, but, mute and enraged, he grabbed a large club with which to beat La Calixta so as to release his fury. After the first two blows, the woman fell, but Calixto continued beating her mercilessly. He would have killed her had he not also passed out on the floor.

They had robbed him of his jewels, which he always carried with him in a pouch sewed into the lining of his trousers. Calixto always believed that it was the fence and his mysterious client.

"What good would the jewels really have been to me," he was now thinking, "if today I find myself before death and will soon disappear?"

The buzzards were circling above the shipwreck victims.

"That *zopilote*," continued Calixto, staring at one of them, "will land on my head, I can already see it."

It ought to be pointed out that the root of the word *zopilote* is composed of *tzotl*, garbage, and *pilotl*, the act of lifting or picking up.

The shipwreck victims were garbage, terrifying garbage:

Hacíamos de cuenta	We understood
que fuimos basuras	that we were pieces of garbage
y que un remolino	and that a whirlwind
nos alevantó,	had lifted us up,
y el mismo viento	and the very same wind,
allá en las alturas,	there in the heights,
allá en las alturas,	there in the heights,
nos aseparó . . .	had separated us.

A dubious, humble song, a savage paraphrase of "from dust to dust." Doomed victims of solitude and fate! Garbage that flies and burns up, a bird, a wing of humble origins!

There were no people greater than those four shipwreck victims tortured by both resentment and hope. There they were, standing guard over their corpse, their tiny Chonita, their great, profound death of garbage with a soul!

"It's already got its eye on me," Calixto was continuing, "and the cursed buzzard won't be long in swooping down on me."

It was a *zopilote* in the middle of the slowly deliberate, graceful, and enemy circle of the other *zopilotes*.

First contemplating from high above, they began swooping down, and one of them, like this one, was flashing its frozen, intent serpent eyes.

A black object, a piece of wood, was floating in the water.

A piece of wood. A boat.

Marcela cried out:

"Look!"

It was floating slowly, calmly, driven by a whimsical breeze.

It stopped in front of the shipwreck victims. A piece of wood. A piece of tree.

"It's Adán, it's Adán!"

A boat, a death, Adán killed by a very clean, horrible knife stab in his throat, behind his ears.

Everyone turned to look since this was so unexpected. But of all of them it was Ursulo alone who totally understood the presence of Adán, the enemy, dead and vanquished. It nevertheless hurt him to see him, as if he were unable to resist that truth, that memory.

Ursulo opened his eyes wide and a fog began to take possession of his brain. "Adán, Adán, it's Adán." Now he was remembering the priest bestially stabbing him and then hiding his eyes in the night.

He tried to speak: "It was when Chonita died, and the priest, for some reason . . . ," as if the crime had taken place a thousand years before.

But once again day was coming to an end and everything would soon be sinking into the desolate shadows.

IX

It was sailing very slowly, prodded by the slight breeze, and it passed before them as if it were a vessel of shadows, an impossible courier.

It was the enemy.

Neither pity nor compassion could move them on his behalf. Today, in this hour of their own shipwreck, they saw their implacable pursuer defeated. His chest and head were floating by, protruding out of the water. The clean wound in his neck, behind his ear, was simply an innocent, bloodless cut, as if painted on. Except for its terrifying face, it was difficult to imagine how that body could be that of a corpse: it had a certain supernatural animation about it as if it had not completely died.

Adán: as he stood there before him as before a necessary, predetermined embankment, Ursulo imagined him to be an enemy ship, resurrected there beside Chonita, growing in the form of livid, uncontrollable ivy. An absurd hallucination flashed and vibrated in Ursulo's mind: Adán would now leap from his own corporeal frame and take his place on the roof. He is now like a zoological vegetable, in the transition that once took place from vegetable to animal, during which time branches began to feel, capable of hate or love or insanity.

Adán was ivy with thoughts and with lips, ceaselessly extending his body, while sap and blood ran together in his vertebras. He had grown in such a way, already master of the celestial vault, that he could have been like an eye seen from the inside, from inside the dark cerebral box with its membranes and its red roots, amid voices that now were calling to Ursulo: "Ursulo, Ursulo!" voices he could not locate in space while a map of yellow membranes and continents, with islands that wounded and furious microorganisms, kept pounding in his brain like obscure galloping.

The sensation was so strange that Ursulo could do nothing short of asking himself whether this was death, whether this was his own death.

He had fallen down, hitting his head hard, and blood reached his brain in intermittent spurts. "It can't be, I don't want to die," he insisted, even though he had known that he was doomed and would be the first to die ever since he had understood that Cecilia would never belong to him again, not even during these last seconds of his life.

In front of him a woman, two women, were leaning over his body.

Cecilia noticed how Ursulo was parting his lips slightly, to utter someone's name. On her knees, she caressed his forehead with a sudden fear that that body would soon be extinguished.

"Leave him alone!" cried Calixto, seeing how Ursulo had become the object of attention and suddenly assuming the role of leader. "Leave him! There's nothing we can do for him."

She turned, ugly and near death, to look at Calixto. The end was approaching for all of them and she could not reply, understanding, just as Calixto had ordered, that this was the way it had to be.

Ursulo's extremely weak breathing was like that of a sick child.

"Will he suffer a lot?" asked Marcela, receiving no answer.

Shadows were swooping down all around them. A strange burst of wind produced a whirlpool inside of which spun Adán, rocking himself only to be still afterward.

Adán, father of Abel, father of Cain, father of men.

That body inhabited by death represented something absolutely significant. This was not an accidental body, but a profound one; this was a somber development.

One year earlier, they had offered that same Adán, that same body that was then inhabited, that same body alive with soul and flame, one hundred pesos for Ursulo's death. And now there he was.

The governor's aide was in Adán's house that day. He was a robust, tall man, with black eyes. His set of teeth was adorned with two magnificent gold caps, there for no other reason.

Adán was cutting his toenails with a large hunting knife on that occasion, after his woman had washed them and for some reason was waiting behind him, in a corner.

Sitting barefoot on the small stool, he was looking attentively at his two clean, dark, tough-skinned feet. Thick callouses preserved his heels, and although they were wide and open-toed his feet remained firm and painless in shoes. The curve of his arches was not very high, which turned his feet into two rootlike, flat masses.

The aide's shadow fell over them.

"*Buenos días!*"

Adán did not raise his head. He had recognized the voice and he turned around only after several moments, and he did so slowly.

"How's it going? Have a seat."

The man's eyes were black and quite agitated. They twitched from right to left, examining everything very quickly, but with astounding precision, not at all superficially.

"What brings you around here?" Adán asked, returning to his toenails.

The man hesitated somewhat.

"Just came by to say hello and see what's new."

Adán outlined an ironic smile.

"Well, as you can see, here I am cutting my toenails."

The aide was wearing a chamois jacket, which seemed to be of very good quality. Adán became uncomfortable and hot in his immediate admiration for it.

"So, what's up?" he asked with a kind of insolence, his eyes still glued to the jacket. "Does my general have something to say?"

"Yes, yes he does," answered the aide, looking at Adán stubbornly.

Both men knew what the general had to "say," but perhaps a tinge of decency or conscience prevented them from speaking.

Adán put on a pair of green socks, and remained shoeless.

His feet resembled those of the statues in the small village churches who wore only green or purple or pink socks on their feet.

The two men looked at each other, harboring the same mutual thoughts of contempt and fear. This had all better be over with as soon as possible.

The governor's envoy rotated the thick belt holding up his pants to the left so that his forty-five pistol became quite visible resting on his thigh. Adán pretended not to give it the slightest thought, but he, in turn, indifferently took his *machete* from the hook where it was hanging and began to play with it.

"My general is fed up with what is going on here in the System," said the aide. "First, the agitation instigated by José de Arcos, Revueltas, Salazar, García, and other communists. Then, that leader, Natividad. And now, once more."

That was simply a prologue. He never told him: "We want you to kill So-and-So." There was just an insinuation: "We don't like So-and-So; and neither does the general. Look, take this money."

Consequently, Adán would later go to the designated place and squeeze the trigger of his gun.

There was something routine in the aide's voice, and Adán became distracted, thinking about other things. This business about the communists was really of little importance to Adán since his role was limited to arresting them and lending his modest assistance for them to be sent to the Islas Marías penal colony. The case of Natividad, of course, was much more serious.

Natividad had an open, wide, magnificent smile. There was something attractive in his face that inspired immediate friendliness. Maybe it was his brilliant, black eyes; maybe his calm, smooth forehead. Adán spoke with him twice. The second time after he had already contracted to kill him.

"Here he comes," he said to himself that second time.

It was still afternoon and the light, as if solid and alive, was pouring down in absolute silence. All along the dull meadow, the farther away a thing was the more sharply it was perceived. A small bush in the distance became a full grown tree, and Natividad had a strange stature, in perfect harmony and proportion, as he walked.

Adán cocked his revolver, getting himself ready.

That meeting seemed all but impossible, and a movement as simple as that of drawing his gun from its holster became difficult for him.

"Hi, Adán. How are things going?" sounded Natividad's strong, confident voice.

Adán moved to one side of the road. "Now, as soon as he gets close," he thought, but his pistol, on his hip, had become dead and useless.

Natividad stopped with his hands on his belt, without apprehension, his eyes smiling.

"You'll never be able to kill me," he said firmly, still smiling, since he already knew of Adán's objectives.

Adán clenched his teeth, lacking the will or energy to attack. Even if he fired, the bullets would not touch that man, and even if they touched him they would not cause him any harm; he was so powerful and confident.

For some reason, Adán felt that this reasoning, so absurd and illogical, was correct. He could not kill him and this was due to a series of reasons beyond his control.

"It'll happen another time, brother," he replied nevertheless. "Be cautious and don't go out alone."

Natividad's eyes grew dark for a second.

An idea, flapping its black wings, had just crossed his mind.

"Unless by treachery," he whispered to himself.

But that was all over in an instant. The shadow dissipated immediately, and Natividad continued on his way with the smile once again on his lips.

There was a particular tone in the meadow that made Adán feel no desire to take up his trek. The vividness and clarity of the air were announcing a change in life. Pink and opal-colored tones poured down gracefully in successive layers or blended together, and the sun's rays were unbelievably thin, dazzling needles. Natividad's figure had disappeared into the next decline, and everything—the very pure light, that autumn of the day right before dusk, the ripe fruit atmosphere—

all contributed to Adán's experiencing the sensation of his failure more strongly.

He had not been able to do anything against Natividad; the solid pistol remained motionless in its leather case and now it became absolutely impossible for him to forget either Natividad's smile or those prophetic, sad words: "Unless by treachery."

He was not afraid of him, he thought, in order to console himself; and even the words that he had actually said to him: "It'll happen another time, brother. Be cautious and don't go out alone," surely indicated his outright, undisguised intentions to kill him. But the real problem—it occurred to him in contrast to his previous thoughts—had nothing to do with his private intentions but, rather, with the concrete, vivid, absolutely real circumstances under which he would kill him. Now, after having seen Natividad face to face, and, especially, after having failed in his attempt to kill him, he felt a kind of imprecise terror, not because of the danger involved, but, rather, simply because he needed to face these circumstances with a vigorous, decisive spirit.

"Unless by treachery," he heard the words again and all he could do was picture his future victim's face momentarily saddened, with a melancholy smile.

"By treachery," he repeated to himself, and a serene conviction had him mutter abruptly:

"Yes, that's the only way."

He continued on with his march, walking in the opposite direction to that taken by Natividad and, in this way, the sun, which was beginning to go down, remained at his back. A peculiar phenomenon developed therefore in front of him. Falling on the small and distant houses before him, the sun's rays gave them extraordinary perfection and plasticity, as if dawn were about to break behind them. Suddenly, twilight began to lose its position, and an incredible dawn, opposite the setting sun, was changing his conceptions of reality. Walking with the sun to his back was, paradoxically, going to meet it, and man could follow this senseless illusion, heading, not to his salvation, but, rather, to darkness, not to the vibrant, creative day, but, rather, to the night of fear and blindness, and all the while believing himself to be in search of light.

Adán walked confidently, unaware of the deception.

The discovery that Natividad could only be killed by treachery profoundly shook his soul: his victory was based on killing and in no way at all on the way he killed, and if for some reason he appeared at first doubtful and defeated it was only because he believed for a moment that *it was impossible* to hurt him. But when he discovered that there was in fact a way—cold and treacherous ambush—his spirit was filled with a soothing, confident calm.

How was he not going to believe, therefore, that, despite the hour of twilight, the sun would appear behind the houses, an evening-daybreak sun that would rise, majestic and solitary now that his soul was calm and ready as never before for whatever miracle?

He walked more briskly but something made him change his course; there on the bridge was a group of men whom he had not wanted to run into.

They were singing a plaintive tune, and without noticing Adán's sudden change of direction, barely a few meters away, they continued nostalgically dragging out the notes made longer and sadder by the gentle afternoon wind.

Their collective face was severe and serious, but at the same time full of confidence. Crowded around a tractor blocking entrance to the bridge, you could see in their faces the profound conviction of their importance and function. Gathered there with their tenacity and commitment, they were the representation of collective force and will. Their simple act of standing there motionless beneath the red flag meant the total paralysis of work in the Irrigation System. Other identical groups, with identical tractors—heavy, animallike, and rhythmic Fordsons—at each bridge over the drains and canals, made up the precise network of the general strike that had broken out a month earlier. The System was actually imprisoned within the metallic, rigid mesh of the network and, without man's labor, the parched land began to bleach and the young cotton plants perished surrounded by ashes.

The unpleasant meeting with these men completely transformed Adán's emotions. Dejection and anguish took hold of his being. The shadows of twilight were slowly falling all around him, like leaves from a celestial tree, depressing him. He was struggling as if against a brick wall, because this was all actually a wall, with the blind, obstinate multitude that seemed immortal.

Adán noticed that among everything against which he was struggling there was one adversary that would never be defeated. What was it? He was unable to answer, but it was absolutely clear that the presence of the strikers gave rise in his spirit to the question and the uneasiness that were making it difficult for him. "What?" he thought. "I'll kill Natividad tonight or tomorrow. But afterward it will be as if Natividad were still alive. They'll make me kill the next one that follows and then the next."

When it came time to kill Ursulo and he could see the aide's face, with its black, cautious eyes and gold teeth, and hear those words "my general is fed up with what is going on here," Adán could do no less than close his eyes as if he were trying to remember something he had forgotten long ago. "All right," he thought harshly, "the Natividad affair is over, but it is as if Natividad were still alive."

He reasoned in this way not because it was repugnant to him to commit new crimes, but, rather, because the crime that would finally ensure him his victory, that firm, complete, sure sensation of power and superiority, had not yet arrived. "Whose turn will it be today?" he asked himself, nevertheless. Perhaps that next homicide would be the one that would grant him his freedom, the one to provide him finally with the exact and unattainable opportunity for which he longed. Possessed suddenly with a burning interest, he leaned toward the governor's envoy awaiting his words.

The aide looked around the room with those same distrustful eyes.

"It has to do with some guy named Ursulo," he whispered.

In spite of the fact that he knew Ursulo very well, no matter how hard he tried Adán could not recall his figure or face. Ursulo's wife had just given birth, and this vaguely bothered him, to the extent that Ursulo seemed even more shadowy, as if he had at most simply seen him in his dreams.

Ursulo was the owner of fifteen hectares of land. Adán could already see him fall, and he could see Cecilia too, as with Natividad, running with her long hair flying. He tried to feel hatred, but he managed only confused reactions of displeasure and irritation. Nevertheless, there was actually a certain interest: for example, would the man be able to cry out or what? In other words, he was interested in the eternal enigma of knowing how a human being responds in the face of death, that seductive, magnificent occurrence that attracts with such immense power.

"All right," he replied.

The aide put fifty *pesos* on the chair.

"The other fifty," he said, "when the job's done."

With her hair flying, like an immense banner that the wind made endlessly longer, Cecilia would once again, as when Natividad was killed, run senselessly, her eyes ablaze. Adán would have to kill her too so that he could raise his status to that of only child, only begotten son, solitary and wretched.

That abysmal vertigo to which he had grown accustomed took hold of him again. It was the same vertigo that possessed him before each and any crime; the sickly tendency to stare into the abyss while summoning absolute, categorical entities and touching upon regions prohibited to the spirit.

When the aide had left, Adán felt like a different person, proud and strong. Today he was a player at the most fantastic gambling table. Elements of an extraordinary nature were being forged in his innermost being from materials that transcended man himself: blind violence, mastery over destiny, and the capacity for limitless destruction. He thus represented the role of fate, not only his offering of himself as executor of its designs but also his acting as fate incarnate and alive, with a creative and destructive will, with the crucial minute in his hands, the all-powerful instrument of the highest and most inconceivable sovereignty.

He heard the grave voice of his woman behind him:

"They're going to kill you," she said apprehensively and gently.

Adán turned his head. He knocked the woman down with a powerful blow.

The woman got up, hiding her bloodied lips with her hand. Indifferently and without uttering the slightest word, she went to the corner of the room, where she sat down composed and serene.

They called her La Borrada because of her cloudy, blue-green eyes, so unusual on that intensely dark-skinned face. Beastly and savagely beautiful, she remained in the corner with the supernatural presence of a violent goddess. She was an Indian woman, perhaps with some non-Indian blood through one of her ancestors, who had been given to Adán by a mountain chief when Adán was municipal agent in the indigenous camps.

After the War of the Cristeros, Adán's protectors had rewarded him with this position so he could hide out for a while far away from the revenge that his innumerable enemies had sworn against him. Adán remained in the mountains for a certain period of time, therefore, more or less at peace.

The indigenous people were not bloodthirsty, cruel, nor rebellious; on the contrary, they were spiritless, sad, hardworking, peaceful, and terrified. They constituted a fraction of a numerous people humbled and destroyed by governments and, perhaps fearing new persecutions, they opted today for submission and humility.

Adán arrived in the mountains one calm afternoon. Without getting off his horse, with the barrel of his pistol he beat the bar that served as a bell to summon the people together. The bar hung in a grove that was evidently the most important spot for the congregation of some twenty families.

Adán was accompanied by five soldiers assigned him by order of the chief of the military zone, so he could "take possession."

Frequently, the soldiers who are ordered to perform their service in remote areas possess very poor and old supplies. Their short jackets, buttonless and the old olive-green almost faded white, already have something civilian about them. Lacking canvas leggings, which have become useless, they tie their riding pants with very poor ixtle fiber or else they leave them loose, thereby exposing their blackened legs where insect bites leave violet-colored stains.

The men accompanying Adán did not even wear shoes. Crude huarache sandals, bound with rough leather straps, served to protect the bottoms of their feet from the coarse earth.

They felt an automatic respect for and an unquestioning submission to Adán, and they were incapable of challenging his authority as leader. Utterly resigned they would comply with whatever order he gave, without a second's thought. They did not really look like soldiers, with their peasant demeanor and their dark, bronzed faces. All of a sudden, removed from large population centers, and in the middle of the mountains, they began to recover their innate sense of the land, asking questions about the type of crop and the type of cultivation, and they themselves, humble once again, sometimes helped in simple farm chores.

Nevertheless, when they appeared at the ranch in the company of Adán—he on horseback and they, behind him, not in any particular order or formation—the indigenous peoples refused to come out. They had been waiting for their appearance for a few hours, ever since the news had reached them by some rather mysterious conduits; it is indeed strange how the wind or perhaps even the plants—it is difficult to believe that it could be man—transmit events in the highlands.

The settlement suddenly became like an abandoned, lifeless village. There were not even traces of fire in the chimneys, nor the usual dirty little children in the doorways, not even dogs. It was a desolation, a silence of abandonment, which nevertheless had something secret and alive about it, as if hundreds of eyes were invisibly watching.

"Good afternoon!" shouted Adán, beating the rail furiously.

The sound was strident and unpleasant. It was metallic; obviously the passing of time had given it a different tone, as if a body, capable of feeling and crying with wretched screams, were being beaten.

Adán noticed that the barrel of his gun had been somewhat damaged by his pounding on the rail, so he put it back in his holster.

"Gabriel," he said to one of his men, "give me that rock," and he pointed to a smooth, round rock at his horse's hoofs.

Sounding that unusual bell was therefore a living hell. The hard, solid rock added another property to the sound, accentuating its ring, which flayed the nerves as if they were being skinned.

"I'll burn down their houses if they don't come out," thought Adán, without seriously intending to do so. Nevertheless, he imagined how he would dismount and head toward the best and largest shack, which was actually right there in front of him, with walls of dry clay made solid with sticks and a cone-shaped straw roof. The fire would consume the straw and then spread with violence. Later the settlement, covered with smoke and flames, would simply remain on the mountain as a black mark from which would emanate that indefinable pungent odor of grain, spicy and charred cereal and wheat ashes.

As a last testimony, however, that sonorous piece of rail would remain, certainly in substance the child or sibling of fire itself, and in any case equally superior and unyielding.

"If you don't come out," shouted Adán, "we'll burn the village."

He then repeated the sentence in the indigenous tongue, which, perhaps because of the whistling and broken melody of the language, showed absolutely no anger. The vowels, amorphous when pronounced separately, took on a rhythm of symmetry and grace when he spoke, thanks to the consonants t, l, and x, which were distributed with musical persistence.

"We'll burn the village!"

When he heard the piercing clanging of the rail, which felt as if he were hearing it through teeth pounded with pliers, Onofre, one of the soldiers, remembered his dog Gazul, who had suffered so terribly when he heard the trumpeting of the bugles. Whenever he heard the sharp, vibrant notes, the poor animal would roll over on the ground in convulsions, howling pathetically. That was in the morning, at four-thirty, during the call to the colors; and then right afterward at five, during reveille, whose initial somber, drawn-out notes soon became a noisy, lively tempo at the deafening sound of the drum roll, the drumsticks alternating between the drum head and the wood casing. Then came the tolling for assembly call, for news reports, and likewise, almost non-stop, for hospital call, ranch call, orders call, the call to quarters, until finally the tolling concluded with the always melancholy and startling taps, at nine o'clock at night.

On one occasion, it seems that Gazul overdid it a little in his reactions. It was one of those magical afternoons in Mexico City, in which you could make out the spreading and partially concealed sun throughout the entire acoustic magnitude of the valley, a resonance box for the miraculous radiance of the hour.

The battalion was lining up in the largest of the two patios of the mess hall, and above the wall could be seen the sober structure of an adjacent colonial church. Any church, even the most humble in the country, offers the vivid and powerful vigor of its principal, majestic structure. Hurling its firm shadow on the patio, over the barracks, the church dome represented the profundity and the silent, surprising sense of beauty that is to be found in Mexico, the unexpected regulator of all things, humble and definitive.

The official, named Marquez, endowed with an immense goatee that fell gently over his brass neck plate, was reading the order, standing in the center of the patio. His voice was energetic and shrill, but Gazul, extremely affected by the bugle call even after it had stopped, thrashed about howling loudly, preventing the officer's words from being heard.

Onofre, from the ranks and in spite of standing rigidly at attention, signaled the dog to be quiet, now moving the fingers of his right hand for him to calm down, as if he were a person, now winking at him, pursing his lips, and softly muttering.

Onofre loved his dog very much and greatly admired his two eyes, one light yellow and the other dark brown. If one looked only at the yellow eye, Gazul's face had something fierce and choleric about it, while the brown eye radiated infinite gentleness and meekness.

"Gazul, Gazul," continued Onofre very softly. "Shut up, they'll punish you," but the animal did not understand his master's anguish.

The official interrupted his reading:

"Sergeant!" he said very calmly and without changing his expression. "Hang that dog!"

A shudder of surprise and sorrow ran through the battalion at this unexpectedly drastic measure, as if the dog were a human being. The soldiers' faces turned to witness the snaring and execution of Gazul, and when the dog was finally hanging from a high beam beneath the shelter of the barracks, the official continued with the reading of the orders, as if nothing whatsoever had taken place.

The rail of the indigenous settlement resonated in Onofre's nerves just as the bugles did in Gazul's. "We are alike in this way," he thought nostalgically.

He had not wanted to hear for another minute the piercing notes that the now furious Adán was arousing from the rail. "Poor Gazul!" he continued thinking, more for his own sake than for the dog's. But at that moment a hunch-backed man began to stumble toward them.

Adán threw down the rock and veered his horse suddenly toward the man.

He was a sturdy, mature Indian who stood completely straight when he met Adán.

"What do you want, *patroncito*?" he asked in his soft, sing-song Spanish.

Searching under his sheepskin jacket, Adán brandished the document that he had brought with him.

"The government has sent me," he said.

The Indian, who was obviously familiar with such matters, astutely inquired:

"And which one of the three governments, *patrón*?"

He was alluding to the municipal, state, and federal governments, and Adán, understanding as much, replied immediately:

"All three together. Look at the order," and he held out the white sheet of paper.

The Indian took the document cautiously. He unfolded it slowly and, after first cleaning his hands on his gray, cotton shirt, he began to read it.

He knew from experience the enormous importance of government papers. Even on the settlement, several large, yellow documents, with handwriting so elegant and beautiful that no one could read it, were preserved with superstitious respect. Only one large number was understandable, apparently indicating the year, 1758. The Indians knew these papers by the name of "property," and it was possible that they were the titles issued by the Spaniards after the *encomiendas* had been abolished.

Everything could be expected from official papers: both good and evil, although almost always evil. During periods of forced recruitment, for example, a group of soldiers under orders of an officer would come to a village. Then the officer would read a government paper and immediately the men were carried off to war, like animals.

The Indian read the document with great care. When he had finished, his tiny eyes flashed again.

"Yes, it must be correct," he said, "especially when you bring soldiers with you. Get down off your horse and come and eat some beans."

Things were going well and they would continue going well. The Indians were unable to rebel, because they were tired of the struggles they had waged so often in previous times, and, when they saw Adán up close, he did not seem to them intolerable in the slightest.

While Adán and his men were eating beans that first day, the indigenous chief, Gregorio, made the housing arrangements: a separate dwelling for Adán and another for the five soldiers.

Afterward, both Gregorio, the chief, and Adán walked along the mountain stream. A woman was bathing there, naked, her long black hair leaning into the water. When she heard their footsteps, she raised her face without the slightest fear, staring at Adán's face with her green-blue eyes. Adán trembled unintentionally.

"How beautiful Borrada is!" he exclaimed.

Gregorio did not react in the slightest, but at dusk, when Adán was lying in his hammock looking toward the door, the woman suddenly appeared.

Adán stood up, surprised.

"What do you want?"

The woman's strangely disquieting eyes looked at him with singular violence, not out of hatred, but, rather, because that is simply what they were: savage and primitive.

"Gregorio told me that I am going to be your woman," she said, "and here I am."

La Borrada was an inscrutable, obscure woman. Her intensely dark face was made up of noble, perfectly harmonious and at the same time solemn lines; it was a face of unexpected dignity, the product of the secret pride that ran through her veins. Lacking refinement as well as harshness, her features revealed a kind of ancient solemnity, as if the woman were the daughter of great lords, or gods, or noble ancestors.

Perhaps Malintzín had been like that: her body perfectly proportioned and in possession of that mysterious disposition so as to give herself to the outsider. Also, as perhaps for the Malintzín of her compatriots, she was treated with superstition and fatalism. La Borrada was the last sign, the door through which they all would pass to another life.

"He's bound to sleep with her," thought Gregorio, when he noticed Adán's stares that first day when they ran into La Borrada. "In any case, he'll sleep with her, just as before, when the Spaniards arrived." He was not her father; La Borrada had no parents.

That is why later he went up to her:

"Your husband has come," he told her.

"That man?"

Gregorio nodded yes.

The moment of her surrender had arrived and La Borrada began to meditate. Everything was being consummated and the pure water of the earth was being buried in the depths of the immense god that is the sea.

"But I don't want children!" she rebelled.

"Don't have them, God willing."

Frightened and possessed with dark foreboding, Gregorio had pronounced these words containing his most burning desires. If La Borrada had a child, that child would become the earth itself resurrected as a wolf, and, once again, there would be the living serpent, the empress serpent and the blood renewed with another, rare venom.

The marriage ceremony was conducted with melancholy, monotonous, quiet, and bitter joy.

When it was discovered that Malintzín was pregnant, the kneeling tribes touched with their foreheads the infinite dust from which they had been born.

"In no way can you prevent my going; I am being forced to go," said Quetzalcoatl at the time, and he concluded: "they have come to call me and the sun calls me."[*]

He then made a raft of snakes and set sail on the sea, with the uncertain destiny of dawn, toward that eternal mystery of the ever nostalgic site of Tlapallan.

Their foreheads sank small oval hollows in the dust that later hardened with the nocturnal time that followed.

Giant churches, like fleshy agave plants made of stone, emerged from their foreheads and the rains began to fall, the cloak of tears began. The priests, walking on their *ixcuintle* skin huaraches and with trembling hands, looked up at the sky.

Where was Tlapallan, column, wind, new rose? Where its gardens of fruit and its countenance?

Malintzín was the mystery and the door, the arch. Under her skin the new waters would rise.

All the tribes, the Olmecs, Tepanecs, Xochimilcas, Tarascos, Mixtecs, and Zapotecs, bowed their heads so they would not be seen, burying them in the earth.

Something was abandoning them. A last star cut through space, without leaving a trace.

After the wedding, La Borrada regularly frequented Doña Demetria's house, where she would ingest strange potions and remain for some time. It was essential that she prevent any descendants.

Whenever she returned to Adán's side her eyes were once again vacant and calm.

[*](Fray Bernardino de Sahagún, 1500?–1590, *Historia general de las cosas de Nueva España*.)

"With this no Indian child will be born," Doña Demetria would repeat, as she prepared the potion. "With this a child will not be born."

Later, in the afternoons, while the sun was going down, La Borrada would lean over to wash her husband's feet. She used a large gourd of sufficient capacity. It was therefore something like a liturgical, antediluvial rite in which the woman caressed Adán's hard, burning feet in her hands.

That afternoon Adán looked at her thick neck bent over the gourd. It was like the knot of a tree along which her black hair, a voluptuous climbing vine, or a capillary forest of dark honeysuckle, ascended.

The woman raised her eyes:

"When you went to the mountains," she said with resentment in her voice, "Gabriel wanted to play with me."

The word *play*, with its precise, intentional accent, was merely a way of establishing the fact that Gabriel, one of the soldiers, had wanted to possess her.

"Is that so?" Adán asked furiously, pushing her away from him with his foot. He got up but all he did was stop at the door, somber and obstinate, to look at the mountain.

"So it was Gabriel, right?"

What kind of surrender or absolute submission was this woman's in which all boats had been burned with no possibility of ever returning to their point of departure? A line drawn in the air but, at the same time, the indelible thickness of a furrow, La Borrada did not exist as categorically as either her presence or her abandonment. Malintzín of earth was again on earth. Nevertheless, there beside him she belonged to him more than anything, and as if for centuries without end.

The next morning Adán sat at the door of the shack, silent and pensive.

Standing on a primitive wooden ladder, Onofre was dismantling the iron rail from the branch. His discovery could not have been more interesting or important. The rail was hanging from the branch with wire, but in such a way that there was not even the slightest space between it and the branch itself. The wire had already dug into the bark, and the rustiness of the rail and the fact that it was so tightly tied to a material that would not vibrate muffled its sound, giving it that irritating tone. All he had to do was lower the rail at a certain distance from the branch in order to recover its former resonance.

Onofre was finishing his task when he heard Adán's voice behind him:

"Gabriel!"

Gabriel had left the shacks heading toward Onofre. Onofre turned his face also, and in one second he managed to witness a clear, real, obvious, and incredible event. When the summoned Gabriel turned fully around, Adán, as if in a dream, took aim with his pistol with astonishing slowness.

Adán was smiling, or so it seemed, but in any case his eyes glistened with joy in the middle of his face.

Onofre believed he heard the noise the bullet produced when it entered the flesh more clearly than the shot itself, as if a small stone had fallen on a bed of moist sand.

Gabriel, having fallen to the ground, twisted convulsively while a reddish blood poured out from his body.

Adán got up from his chair and with equal slowness, as if it were difficult for him to walk—he was obviously struggling to repress a violent and undefined emotion, which was not fear, but, rather, perhaps limitless consternation and astonishment—he approached the wounded man and nudged him with the tip of his foot.

"Come here, Onofre," he said softly, as if he were in church.

His lips were as white as flour but his face did not show the slightest trembling, and not a single wrinkle moved.

Onofre dismounted.

"Get your gun!"

One of Adán's feet was resting on the wounded man's stomach.

"Finish him off!"

He tried to add "And be careful" because it occurred to him that the coup de grace might absurdly splash blood over his trousers.

Onofre lifted the rifle to his face and aimed at the wounded man's temple.

"Forgive me, little brother!" he said, because Gabriel was his friend and because at that moment Gabriel's eyes were staring at him, expressing a certain terrifying entreaty. Then he fired.

One second later, having climbed to the top of the ladder, Onofre was able to verify that the iron rail rang solemnly, swinging in large and deep sonorous circles.

From that moment on, an illogical sadness took possession of Adán.

Gabriel's death was, in a certain way, the first he had consummated on his own initiative and this fact produced in him a kind of terror, as if he had been told that his own will and judgment were now dominated by some monster and no longer existed at all. He had therefore believed himself to be something like an executor of fate, marginal to things and possessor of a clear independence, but suddenly he began to understand that his soul was a leaf lost in the storm, without the slightest anchor, jostled about capriciously and totally lacking in free will.

The fact that he had ordered Onofre to fire the coup de grace—instead of Adán himself executing his revenge including its final consequences—was the recognition that something was beginning to rise up before him, forcing him to surrender to it. For the first time he had been afraid to kill, even when it seemed rather simple and uncomplicated. A strange terror began to be born and from that time on he would live enslaved, expecting at any minute to be hurled into the final abyss.

Long days and endless months went by in which Adán, swinging in his hammock, did nothing else but remain absorbed in monotonous, obstinate thoughts.

"You've got jaundice," La Borrada would tell him, standing behind him caressing his neck. "Yes, that's what you've got."

Doña Demetria's herbs, however, had not proved helpful, nor had the still half-alive, bleeding animal carcasses that she had split open and rubbed on his chest, over his heart.

Adán finally decided to leave the cursed settlement. He saddled his horse and left followed by La Borrada, on foot.

"I'll send a replacement," he told his soldiers.

A while afterward, Adán's protectors entrusted him with the death of Natividad, but not without first reprimanding him for Gabriel's useless, vain death. When he had explained the details to them, however, both the governor and the chief of operations agreed with him. The governor affirmed sententiously: "a woman, a horse, and a gun are sacred."

But the problem now was Natividad, a leader. They in no way intended the strike of five thousand farm laborers to continue, a scandal for the Republic and even for the revolution itself. "Natividad, Natividad." He had dark eyes and a profound expression; he was strong and active. Adán shuddered recalling Natividad's beautiful, noble face.

"Fine!" he murmured timidly before his superiors.

The strange emotion that Adán felt toward Natividad ever since he had received the order to kill him was caused by Natividad's fortitude, honor, and characteristic human solidity. A confusing feeling overcame Adán when he perceived his actual impotence before a man so powerful and confident. It seemed as if he were confronting an immortal being whose reasons for living were superior to life itself.

"I won't be able to do it," he thought.

And he would not be able to do it simply because of his memory of the first time he had spoken with Natividad.

Natividad was riding that first time toward the houses of the System, astride a gaunt nag whose reddened, melancholy eyes betrayed great exhaustion, like a human being fully resigned to suffering, with skinny legs, and a bony, cadaverous head.

When he saw Adán heading toward him from the opposite direction, Natividad dismounted.

"Good morning."

Adán's primitive suspicions immediately diappeared before the obvious cordiality of the man whom he was meeting for the first time.

"Good morning," he replied, also lifting his hand to his wide-brimmed, straw *sombrero*.

There was a great power of suggestion in that man. He pronounced his words with unusual vigor, discovering interesting aspects in the most trivial questions, which took on new meaning under their common appearance.

"Is this the Irrigation System?" asked Natividad. "I suspected as much from the beginning, even though I thought I was lost. In Nogal, they told me that it was still some distance away."

With his thumbs in his belt, Adán agreed:

"Yes, sir, Nogal is far away."

For Natividad, life was enormously rich and fertile, and any of its details, even the slightest, contained a universe of passion.

"Do you know a day-laborer by the name of Jerónimo Gutiérrez?" he asked.

The tone of the question elevated Jerónimo Gutiérrez, a simple day-laborer, bestowing upon him legitimate dignity and inalienable lineage.

Yes, Adán knew him, but the day-laborer in question did not live in the village, but, rather, some 37 kilometers away, precisely in a place called Thirty-Seven-Six, because of the distance of 37.6 kilometers.

Natividad made a gesture of annoyance. Luckily, it was still early in the morning and if he continued at a brisk pace he could arrive before dark.

Adán felt Natividad's horse's chest as if to calculate its endurance.

"If you don't race the animal," he said, half-convinced and half-skeptical, "at a good pace you can arrive in the cool of the evening."

He offered to accompany him on the same road, since he was going as far as the 25th kilometer, and from there Natividad could go on alone.

They spoke of many matters along the way. The Irrigation System, with its vast extension and its straight, well-designed canals, surrounded them.

The central government, deeply worried about giving its Agrarian Reform program a modern and advanced face, had established in the country different irrigation units on the lands expropriated from the large estates. Rivers with irregular courses were used to construct large dams in which water was stored to be rationally distributed later according to the needs of the farmers. An agency of the Agricultural Bank, in combination with a high-ranking agency of the Ministry of Agriculture, financed the tenant farmers, who paid off the loan by giving over to the bank the product of the land, most of which was destined for the Yankee market. In this way, the government achieved a series of objectives: it established a deeply entrenched, solid, and conservative class of medium-sized property owners with which it moderated the otherwise extremist impetus of the agrarian revolution, while at the same time passing itself off as a government that had not abandoned its principles and that was still able to inscribe on its banners that barbarous motto of "Land and Liberty."

The Irrigation System Corporation was divided simply: large *colonos*, owners of one hundred or more hectares; middle-sized *colonos*, possessors of more than fifty hectares; poor or small *colonos*, owners of fifteen or fewer hectares; and salaried laborers, who served all the others for a salary of thirty, forty, fifty, and up to seventy-five *centavos* a day.

The government was never able to conceal its delight at this experiment, and the revolutionary intellectuals of the epoch wrote erudite articles and profoundly thoughtful theses to communicate to the world the good news about "Mexican socialism." It goes without saying that the government, in turn, actually footed the bill for the "personal works" of these intellectuals, who published, together with the "political" essay, for which they had deep scorn, luxurious *plaquettes* of their poetry and other literary flights, since "hunger," as Cervantes has said, "perhaps inspires geniuses to discover things not on the map."

Natividad was walking with the bridle of his horse in his hand to be on equal terms with his spontaneous companion. A solid, rhythmic, and harmonious sound was rising around them. It was the tractors, which, even if they appeared small in the distance, nevertheless produced their vivid and inspirational murmur. Everywhere work was conducting its virile symphony and one could hear intermittently the day-laborers' voices, full of power and volume, hoarse, piercing, solemn, and vibrant with life. The individual plots of land were superimposed in precise rectangles, whose color varied imperceptibly with the undulations of the terrain, and in the distance they began to turn from grey or green to violet in the morning mist.

Persistent, hoarse bees, buzzing within an absolute calm, that was the noise of the tractors; but one sensed nevertheless in that sound a certain warlike quality, as if machine guns were firing continuous bursts under the concavity of the sky that was ready for anything and full of resonance. This is what happens in war. One can see the sky, the clouds, the green color of the fields, and the only thing that exists is the noise, as if death were so far away. Beyond, on the other side, you can hear the noise, just the noise, and it resembles a muffled march that suddenly and surprisingly stops, only to commence again and stop once more. The air is quiet, still, and one can hear everything clearly: the march of violent feet on the other side of the green hill, at first as if walking slowly, although always in regular rhythm, only to stop later, the bastards! They turn their heads from right to left, sniff the air, and refuse to advance without first feeling totally secure. But suddenly the deaf murmur starts up again and a gigantic drum can be heard: the cannons have returned. When the enemy crosses the green hill and is right here among us on this side, furious and fierce in battle, the panorama is different. Very vivid things begin to happen: a comrade falls; another curses; there is sweat and deathly pale faces. But viewed from up high and from a distance, war is just like the Irrigation System, where the tractors buzz as if they were moving within an unreal, delimited, and secret atmosphere.

Here and there the canals, wounded by the sun, were glistening as if made of silver. Running through the green and violet of the farm plots, therefore, was a knife, a line of joyful metal: the magical gift of the water with its secret flashes of light and its interior stars.

Natividad was intrigued by the land, by the transformation through which it was passing. Before, when mankind came into being, it would not have been like this, so burdened with labor and tears. But today the beloved mother was aging, and they had to bend their bodies and permit sweat to pour from their foreheads.

"How do they work here?" he asked, knowing from experience that methods varied according to the climate and crop.

"Well, first of all, they plow," answered Adán with a soft, nostalgic voice.

(Nevertheless, when seen up close the water was not transparent; but somewhat whitish. A certain foam of saltpeter and harmful substances had formed near the small floodgates of the drains.)

"Then comes the sowing."

(In the long run, this impure liquid could ruin the already naturally poor and hard land which already lacked sufficient phosphates.)

"Then they have to begin to irrigate with great care until the plants have sprouted."

(With abundant fertilizers and the establishment of a system of rotation that allowed the land to breathe, they could nevertheless exploit the land for a longer period of time, since the days of the project's life would otherwise surely be numbered.)

"Later comes the weeding, which leaves the plants clean as a whistle."

(The totally inadequate distribution of property constituted a terrible obstacle for any reform. Perhaps a cooperative and the introduction of collective work would have improved everything.)

"After that comes the first harvest."

(But there were also a bank, politicians, numerous economic interests.)

During the twenty-five kilometers that they traveled together, Adán and Natividad chatted with great animation. Adán, less communicative, expressed himself with reservation and reticence. Natividad, frank and honest, sprinkled his conversation with anecdotes.

One especially remained engraved in Adan's memory.

"It was," began Natividad, "a strange night. Nothing was stirring; everything was frozen and still owing to the excessive gravity of the air which had turned into black lead."

They had been pursuing the enemy for three weeks, without overtaking them. But this, in itself, was not what was so unusual. The strange thing was that no one at all had seen the enemy or knew of their number or their strength. In relentless pursuit of ghosts, the men had become exhausted. For the first three days it all seemed natural enough: "They're afraid of us," they all affirmed. But on the fourth day a slight uneasiness began to spread. The monotony of the pursuit and the constant state of alert gave rise to the wildest stories: the enemy, it was said, did not want to engage in open combat simply because they were organizing an ambush on their own land where they would kill us unmercifully. "There is no such enemy," affirmed one wild explanation; "the thing is that we have all been drugged with the narcotic *toloache* and we're all going crazy." For all its imagination, this explanation was, of course, the one with the most believers. The enemy was a phantom hallucination and this appeared to be the only reality.

Between the fifth and sixth day, a soldier claimed to have seen a squadron of cavalry cross the nearby bridge in perfect formation. He swore that he had seen the helmets of the federal troops, but that they had all disappeared further on in an undulation of the terrain. Since the theater of vision was the moonless evening, the narrators embellished and lengthened that vision each time with new details: for example, that a woman, mounted on a very dark horse and with trappings of mourning, was riding in front of the squadron, white and faceless except for her terrifying and bony cheekbones above her sinister teeth. Others said that it was not a squadron but an entire regiment, against which one could fire without the slightest result.

On the seventh day, an interesting event took place. At about three o'clock in the morning, a gunshot was heard outside the campsite. The troop awoke and an attempt to sound an alarm was quickly suffocated, whereupon a sentinel burst into the camp and did not stop until he was face to face with the commanding officer. The sentinel, a young man of eighteen, was unable to utter a word. With his eyes bulging out of their sockets and as white as paper, he was only able to emit a guttural, awkward sound that expressed nothing, while his pasty tongue emerged from his lips as if it were actually growing and could no longer fit inside his mouth.

That boy would have died from terror if the commander, with two good slaps, had not made him react. As soon as he had come to his senses, he gave a detailed narration of what had occurred, not without first making the sign of the cross.

He was on guard duty, some four hundred meters from the campsite, when he heard the sound of steps. They were not, apparently, the steps of a single person. They appeared instead to be those of a group, and a group of *men*. The sentinel insisted that the steps were precisely those of men: hard, rhythmic, and firm. "It must have been the nightwatch," he thought, since a group of soldiers, under orders of a second lieutenant, performed this service every night. The sentinel uttered the required "who goes there?" and the answer he received left him paralyzed with terror. In the first place, the sound of the steps suddenly ceased, but he immediately heard a terrible and superhuman voice or shriek. It was in no way a common, ordinary voice; it seemed as if an insane, unhinged woman were suddenly possessed by a nameless hysteria which produced the metallic, piercing shriek. Besides, the fact that it had a feminine ring, especially since he had earlier heard men's steps, immediately gave the situation a supernatural character. With great effort, the sentinel bolted his rifle, checking his cartridges. Miraculously, at the conjuration of the noise, the voice stopped dead. As best he could, and trembling at what he had heard, the sentinel squeezed the trigger of his rifle, aiming toward the spot from where the shriek had seemed to come. But imagine his surprise when he discovered that, instead of a shot, his weapon had produced a hollow, deaf sound. As soon as *whatever* it was right in front of him *on the other side* had realized that the gun had not functioned, the voice, lament, or shriek, even closer now and more shrill, could once again be heard. It was an absolutely nonhuman howling devoid of any real physical qualities, and the sentinel felt a cold gust upon his face, cheeks, and then behind his ears. He loaded and fired his gun three times, all with the same result. Finally he managed to get a shot off and then heard a moan and—of this the sentinel could not be absolutely sure—a curse. He forced himself toward the place where he had seemed to have seen a shadow, and there indeed on the ground was some kind of dark body. Nevertheless— and the narration was already taking on a somewhat fantastic dimension—when he touched that alleged body with the barrel of his rifle, a body at times resembling a bundle of clothes according to the sentinel, it had already disappeared, dragging itself away, as if it were being pulled by someone. When it had completely disappeared among the nearby scrubs, the moaning began again, only now from a considerable distance away.

The commanding officer listened to the entire narration and, since he was both a skeptic and a freethinker, arranged later for three men to go to the spot to see if it would be possible to find the mysterious body to which the sentinel had referred.

The three men returned empty-handed, while the sentinel remained under arrest to be shot the next day for "deserting in the face of the enemy."

Where was this enemy? Did they exist or was it all merely a demented and savage illusion?

After ten days of useless pursuit, the commanding officer himself appeared to be losing his mind. They were struggling against a wall of air. Everyone felt blind, insane, hopelessly lost, running in all directions, crashing into closed doors and purposeless.

The commanding officer summoned his officers.

"I have decided," he began, "that we'll wait for the enemy right here. If they really want a fight and don't just want to harass us, they'll come looking for us. We have no other choice. We'll take the necessary precautions."

Assembled under a sturdy, sheltering oak tree, they resembled a small picturesque tribe, one of those passionate tribes that ignited the country during the first days of the revolution. All the officers agreed with their commander since they too were tired and somewhat apprehensive.

The commander was speaking when suddenly something appeared to draw his attention.

"What happened to your hand?" he suddenly said, addressing one of his officers.

The officer in question was a young career military man, the only one among them and among the many more in the entire country, a graduate of the College of Chapultepec who had embraced the cause of the revolution. Because of his military pedigree and his culture, one might say that he was a respectable traditionalist, a disciplined and strict lover of order. No one knew why he was in the revolution.

His face grew pale.

153

"The other day I wounded myself cleaning my pistol," he said.

The purple color of his fingers could be seen between the bandages of his right hand.

"Let's see!" said the commander.

He liked to treat his subordinates paternally, and he drew great satisfaction from helping them and learning about their problems.

"This could cost you your arm, captain," he said when he saw the wound.

The captain's hand was like a ball of rotting flesh.

"Look," said the commander to an orderly. "Go get Natividad; he's good at things like this."

Natividad, at that time, was a driver for the revolutionaries. This was a provisional commission since the vintage Overland that they used to transport plans, telescopes, and staff supplies was not always able to cross the rough terrain. Nevertheless, they needed Natividad for other commissions as well: curing wounded and sick soldiers with herbs or bleedings; attending the pregnant *soldaderas* during birth, with boiling water and presence of mind; and writing communiqués and typing them on the dreadful, prehistoric Oliver. That's why they admired him, and why he was one of the people for whom everyone, without exception, felt that spontaneous gratitude and confidence that are born when in the presence of someone truly useful.

Natividad examined the captain's wounded hand, shaking his head somewhat worriedly. The only treatment the wound had received had been a little water, perhaps not even boiled, and it was not difficult to diagnose blood-poisoning.

He made the captain sit in a chair and he tied him to it tightly with rope.

"Be brave, my captain!" he warned him.

154

His face ghostly pale, the captain nodded by lowering his head, while a choleric spark glimmered in his eyes.

"Where have I seen those eyes before?" Natividad asked himself. He remembered that face, but it was in relation to something unpleasant which he could not pin down. "Where, where?"

The captain conducted himself with absolute courage. Other officers, who were unable to conceal their horror, and even the commanding officer himself were astounded.

Natividad made an incision in the swollen hand so deep that one could see the whiteness of bone. He then squeezed the pus out and poured hydrogen peroxide onto the red flesh which on contact produced a certain white, foul-smelling foam.

The captain, seemingly oblivious to the torture, did not make the slightest gesture. But his face turned more and more pale.

"After another three applications of this cure," said Natividad, "you'll be out of danger."

These words made the captain react as if they had been knife stabs, and he once again showed a flash of intense rage in his eyes, a flash totally his own and unforgettable. "Now I remember!" it suddenly occurred to Natividad, opening his mouth in surprise.

Yes, that refined, handsome face lacking in nobleness, those thin lips, like a dagger's blade, those colorless cheeks, those eyes. The most characteristic part of that face was really the eyes. It was not that they lacked brightness; rather, they feigned not having any. But deep down they were flashing, capable of cruelty and coldness. At first sight, they actually seemed opaque, because he kept them half-closed, as if under the spell of an impossible drowsiness. His paltry, sickly eyelids covered half of his pupils, giving his face a certain hypnotic look. Perhaps that was his way of hiding or faking certain thoughts. In any case, it was difficult to penetrate this man's inner being and secret designs. Was he lying, did he love, did he hate, was he capable of suffering? It was impossible to know.

Natividad had already seen that abrupt eye-movement somewhere else. The indifferent, cold, and soulless eyelids suddenly opened, and then immediately returned to their previous position. In that very instant, the captain's unrevealed spirit burst to the surface, exposing itself as inexorable and fanatic.

The clarity of the dawn was on that occasion already visible on the horizon. A group of five soldiers was escorting the sentinel who had fled his post terrified the night before when pursued by that mysterious moaning which he had heard under such strange conditions in the darkness. It was later said that inside the guardhouse where he was being detained, the young sentinel had slept untroubled, deeply. When a sergeant finally woke him up, it occurred to him to ask what day it was.

"Thursday!" the sergeant answered.

The boy had a pleasurable certainty of his death. It would have been terrible for him to have gone on living after the supernatural trauma he had suffered; so the death sentence appeared to him more as a favor than anything else. That explains his deep, comforting sleep.

"Thursday?" he whispered, as if he were speaking with someone very near or inside of himself. "Any day is fine."

He was smiling a little foolishly, like someone ashamed of something or minimally punished for a mistake deserving of a harsher penalty.

In the campsite, things had gone on as always. Approximately ten soldiers showed a certain curiosity for what had happened and a group of women lingered in front of the doors of the guardhouse.

"They are for his breakfast," explained one of the women, carrying in her basket flour *tortillas* and coffee with milk in a jug with yellow decorations. "The poor thing! How can he go without eating breakfast?"

The event in this way resembled the preparations for a departure or move to another campsite. "How can he go without eating breakfast?" A departure surrounded by tenderness and good-byes without sadness.

Appearing uninterested in the affair, the young captain walked all around the campsite with his head downcast and drowsy eyes. He gave the impression of a sick insomniac who had needed to get up out of bed to distract himself.

What was about to take place was a humble, unceremonious execution by firing squad under the gray dawn. It did not seem possible, right there, with the wall, with the group of *soldaderas*, with the air.

The boy went out escorted by the five guards. The women offered him the basket of *tortillas*, and for a few minutes everything was interrupted; life stood still within the greatest of silences, while the boy ate.

With his innocent face he thanked the women in a quiet, sweet voice, like that of a child.

"Thank goodness!" the women wailed. "How bravely he's going to die!"

The captain remained impassive, walking with his head down as if nothing were happening around him. Nevertheless, he came up to within about ten meters of the wall to watch the execution.

When it took place, and the captain heard the shots, his eyes flashed sinisterly. A spark of immense joy glistened in his pupils.

The people mourned the death of the young sentinel, but there was no one to hate for that death. That was the way things were and that was the way they had to be.

When after ten days of absurd nightmares the commanding officer agreed to set up camp to wait out the enemy, the entire troop was able to rest a while. A feeling of calm seemed to float in the air. Faces began to show a kind of fearlessness, and an order to oil weapons filled the camp with a feverish and joyful activity. The soldiers unbolted their rifles, greasing them with oil and they later seemed pleased with the smooth sound of precision of the assemblage.

In the evenings, they sang *corridos* of war, love, floods, ghosts, crimes, and prisoners. One of the songs told the story of a certain very famous event in the northern mineral region from which it came. The people of that region are sober, serious, trustworthy, and not prone to exaggeration, in contrast to the long-suffering and suspicious character of the Mesa Central.

A silent, curious circle, apparently engrossed in very simple but also profound and emotional memories, began to form around the singer.

> "It was a Sunday, truly,
>
> when it happened that . . . "

The Mexican has a very devout, very deep and respectful sense of his origins, a kind of dark, unconscious atavism. Since he is ignorant of his true origins and retains only a confusing presentiment of them, he constantly suffers from an incurable and persistent nostalgia. So he drinks, or he drinks and sings, harboring the most contradictory feelings, at times furious, at other times deeply saddened. What does he want? What is he thinking when he turns his gaze to the empty horizons, to his ancient, motionless landscape, capable of remaining that way for years perhaps without a single thought crossing his mind? Perhaps he longs for an earthly, original mother and wishes to hear her voice and her call.

"... the young José Lisorio,"

continued the *corrido*.

It was the story of a miner, José Lisorio. He drank frequently, and on one occasion when his mother had scolded him for such behavior, the "young José Lisorio" became enraged

"and he hit his mother."

The mother cursed the perverted miner, and on the very next day he went down into the bottom of the mine only to meet his death in a horrifying cave-in. The moral of the *corrido* tended to exalt the veneration owed a mother. But in no way was José Lisorio's mother tender and sweet. Instead, she was horrible, prophetic, obscure, and filicidal. Untouchable and magical mother of the Old Testament, with powers over destiny, as cherished and silently beloved as a sinister taboo, or a circle, a timeless distance, an impossible line.

It was one of those primeval nights common to our latitude, quiet, motionless, and therefore quite startling, in which one doubts the existence of man and even that of the earth itself. Surrounded by darkness, the spirit abandons itself to an endless wandering, lost, having given up all hope.

Suddenly shooting was heard. In the far distance one could hear shouting but it was impossible to distinguish the human voices from the howling of the dogs.

The men picked up their weapons and suddenly the campsite exploded in a general uproar. Shadows were rushing everywhere, there was mass confusion and everyone began shooting without rhyme or reason.

The four sharp notes of the bugle ordering a "cease fire" miraculously succeeded in returning everything to its previous state.

Yes, evidently it had been a surprise attack. But, the enemy? Where were they? The group that had gone out looking for them had surrendered to a blind, frantic, wild-goose chase. They had run furiously and fearlessly for almost nine kilometers, until the edge of night and the beginnings of morning, finding themselves suddenly facing an abandoned, misty, and solitary plain besieged by the light of the sun. There was no such enemy.

What was to be done when the struggle had no objective, meaning, or reality? They were walking over a vast, deserted country, with the enemy in the air, and everything began to lose its point of relation, especially man, as if he were on another planet and the atmosphere had turned solemn, alien, and intensely hostile.

The commander called his officers together once more. They assembled right there in the wilderness.

They could expect nothing, they thought with total abandon, but the desperate obstinacy of continuing their coming and going from place to place without respite.

There were about eight or ten officers. The revolution still had not provided them with uniforms, dragging them along from place to place with nothing but badges on their wide-brimmed civilian *sombreros*. On their coarse shirts or jackets, two crossed straps indicated that they were revolutionaries, and their faces, except that of the wounded captain, were absolutely those of the people, frank and serious.

This revolution that seemed not to know itself was a curious one. Other revolutions in the world took their slogans and banners from previous revolutions, even from those examples of classical antiquity, and thus became grave, conservative, and redemptive. But this revolution seemed as if it were developing in the center of Africa, its men ignorant of where they and their fathers and grandfathers had begun. Some generals seemed to be participating in the revolution, monetary benefits aside, simply for the pleasure of writing manifestos in the style of Vargas Vila, and the solemn masses that marched behind them were perhaps there only to avenge the death of Cuauhtemoc, whose feet the Spaniards burned during the Conquest. But in any case this revolution was something obscure, concealed as it was within its great profundity.

Zapata was a general of the people, completely of the people. He had no idea where Verdun was. During the War of 1914 he believed, so they say, that the Carrancistas, his enemies, were attacking Verdun. Zapata was of the people, the pure and eternal people, in the middle of a savage and just revolution. Those who were not ignorant of where Verdun was, were ignorant, instead, of everything else. Totally ignorant. And life left them there, their backs up against everything beloved, somber, proud, noble, and sinister that was the revolution.

Eight or ten officers with bronze or brown or black faces, dressed in grimy shirts and pants, except for that polished and impeccable son of Chapultepec.

No one knew why the commanding officer decided to harangue them before getting down to business; perhaps it was his anguish. He spoke to them about ideals, freedom, and the fact that their names would be mentioned in history. In history, that is, in schools, where children would learn about them just as they learned about the priest Hidalgo or the priest Morelos.

Then he got down to speaking about what was on everyone's mind, and the conjecturing increased.

The captain with the wounded hand offered the opinion that the enemy did not have organized and coherent nuclei, but, rather, depended on bands capable of attacking here and there in small skirmishes, albeit effectively enough to plant the seeds of panic and demoralization. The captain explained his theory with such precise detail, as if he himself had actually been informed by the enemy.

Everyone turned toward the captain and unintentionally stared at his wounded hand. Free of the cloth sling, his hand was resting on his thigh, still slightly swollen and with the tips of his fingers yellowish and inflamed.

The commanding officer's eyes also noticed the captain.

Something suddenly seemed disquieting about that man. No one could say precisely what it was, but they all felt that he was a being completely alien to them, with his half-closed eyes and that cold, sober, and cruel logic of which he was capable.

"Nevertheless," the commanding officer continued, and everyone's eyes returned once again to those of their leader, "we have to realize one thing: we are at the mercy of whoever they are and there's nothing we can do but keep walking and walking without respite."

There were two second lieutenants, three lieutenants, two captains, and a few others, all brown-skinned. Some had pock-marked faces; others had gold teeth, almond-shaped, oriental eyes, and pitch-black stiff hair. Only the captain with the wounded hand was light-skinned with neatly trimmed hair.

"What's he up to?" the commanding officer asked himself, unintentionally restless. "What was he plotting with that lizard face of his?" And, then aloud:

"There's nothing else we can do," he concluded, referring back to the eternal subject of their eternal flight.

That group of revolutionary soldiers lost in the immense geography of Mexico had become a group of defeated men in flight. This was not the revolution; it was nothing: it was just walking, walking, walking. Where was the flag? If even one federal soldier had appeared, they would have taken him with them, cut off his feet, and made him walk innumerable kilometers over the fire of the earth, until he died. But, where was the meaning of it all? Where was the earth? Walking, walking without respite.

During that same afternoon the captain came up to Natividad who was leaning over the engine of the car.

"You're going to accompany me," he said, "on a mission."

Natividad stared at him cheerfully:

"At what time?"

"Right now."

They got into the Overland heading in some undefined direction. It was in the afternoon and the harsh sun was bathing the immense wasteland where the maguey plants cast their wide, angular shadows. The sun was painting the earth, the dust, a certain orange color. The Overland's engine vibrated while the old tires sank into the dust. But this entire trip, like the fantastic campaign itself, lacked all meaning. "Where were they going?" Natividad might have wanted to ask of his companion but was prevented from doing so by the drowsy, unfocused eyes staring straight ahead over the hood of the automobile.

They were surrounded by neither horizon nor time, only the terrible loneliness of the maguey plants, astonishingly outlined in the form of dirty green splatterings amid the sun-baked dust.

For two hours they heard only the intolerable sound of the engine, while traveling in a direction known only to the captain.

The engine suddenly stopped cold.

"Wait!" said the captain, and he got out and leaned over the trunk.

The afternoon was coming to an end and it must have been around six o'clock because a flock of birds was crossing the sky rapidly and in panic. Birds over the solitude of Mexico! They were birds of the epoch, birds of that desolate time, stupefied by the noise, the shrieks, and the blood of the earth. Birds that had remained hovering above the revolution observing the corpses, the silence of the guns and all the tiny people so busy in matters of death.

Natividad, in turn, was leaning over the pedals of the Overland to check something, but no sooner had he hidden his head when he heard a blood-curdling, feminine, absurd shriek, and an icy coldness ran down his spine. That was exactly the same thing the executed sentinel must have heard, attributing it to otherworldly beings.

Natividad stared at the pedals and then right above them; the broken contact wire next to the useless speedometer was the cause of the accident. Now Natividad understood: the captain was the cause of everything. He was obviously a spy for the *federales* and was communicating with the enemy, providing them with information and creating that state of intolerable exodus suffered by the revolutionary troops. The sentinel they had later executed must have wounded him in the hand; that must have been the explanation for the captain's joy during the execution. He was a son of Chapultepec, the military school of the Porfiriato. He would never love the revolution.

Many things passed through Natividad's head, in aggressive yellow and electric-blue colors. But there was absolutely nothing he could do because the captain was summoning him from the trunk of the Overland with his pistol.

The captain's eyes were now open with a diabolic fire and could finally be seen to be dark brown, with a blemish of the same color in the white of the eye near the pupil. Besides being an escape valve for his hysteria, that shriek was simply part of some strategy.

"Take this, you son of a drunken whore!" he shouted, squeezing the trigger.

Natividad thought about the young sentinel, that poor kid! about his terror, and about his own terror. The young sentinel had been killed. With five bullets. Six, counting the coup de grace. He had been killed in the early morning, barely a few days earlier, when the red, bleeding sun was announcing its arrival, tinting the white walls. How could one explain the sentinel's grateful face or describe that shyness before death that made him take pity on the spectators while he smiled apologetically? Five shots and six with the coup de grace, which is, indeed, a kind of "grace," a favor, a gift: the bullet that kills, the one that truly annihilates all suffering so that man can pass into the realm without light, time, space, ideas, hands, or eyes, the realm of nothingness. Without eyes to see and without a soul to realize that he sees nothing.

But the captain was white, with the pistol in his hand, senselessly squeezing the trigger of a pistol totally out of cartridges.

Insane with terror, the captain searched his bags. What ensued immediately was a terrifying pursuit.

The captain fell, got up again, seemingly oblivious to the razor-sharpness of the maguey plants, in desperate flight.

"Even if I have to chase you for a thousand centuries," roared Natividad with all his soul, "I'm going to take you prisoner."

Natividad captured the spy at about ten o'clock in the evening, under several million stars. He tied his hands and feet with the *ixtle* fiber he had made by pounding maguey leaves with a stone. And even though he had cut his hands in the process, the captain's hands would be cut too. Then he lay down to rest, intending to head back to the campsite.

One hundred million stars were out: the two Bears, the Dipper, and other constellations to which the people did not give mythological names but, rather, names that had to do with the Virgin Mary and the baby Jesus. They could not get lost, with so many stars, just as the Three Kings, the Virgin Mary, and the baby Jesus had not gotten lost during the flight from Egypt that so extraordinarily tender and fragrant night.

Adán was listening with true amazement, reconstructing in his mind the obscure wilderness under that starry night, the somber maguey plants, and the traitor captain with his head face-down in the dust. There was something fantastic and mysterious in Natividad's story, as if it were a nebulous as well as a profound and disquieting painting.

"And then?" he asked.

Natividad responded first with his active, intense eyes.

"We made it to the car," he continued, "and we went back to the campsite, but there wasn't anyone there any longer. Then it became terrifying. We abandoned the Overland which had run out of gas. We were totally lost. I wanted to crush his skull with a rock, so that he'd finally die and free me, but I couldn't.

They were walking as if they had landed on the moon, wandering over extinct craters, trees of limestone, and a hollow earth.

Natividad was forcing his prisoner to walk, driving him on with stones since he could find no other way. If he only had had one bullet for the gun, it would have been the greatest, most extraordinary thing in the world, but there the machine was, with its intelligent springs, its singular nature, empty, horrifying, and useless in his pocket. With one bullet one could take death's hand and command it: "Make the bastard walk, make him lie down, make him run, make him stop, make him speak, beg, cry."

The captain was walking ahead, his hands tied, and whenever he stopped a stone hit his heels, his legs, his shoulders, or his ribs. A stone instead of the gun, even though with a gun everything would have been less cruel, cleaner, without his heels sounding like solid rubber and his ribs emitting a completely muffled thud.

The captain did not utter a single complaint. He merely tightened his lips.

"You'll see," he said furiously, "when Don Porfirio returns."

"If you're still alive to tell about it," Natividad answered.

The prisoner tried to run away twice, and both times he fell brutally and defenselessly, smashing his face against the stones like a madman.

He began to pray:

"Holy Mary, Mother of God, the Lord is with Thee," and he refused to go on.

Natividad stopped, not knowing what to do. The only logical thing was to kill him. But, how? How could he kill a man without a gun or a knife, with only his teeth and his hands? He could smash his skull to pieces with one of those huge, heavy rocks, but then there was the terrifying doubt that he might not die after the first blow, in which case Natividad would be condemned to weep for centuries and centuries.

"Die, die, you son of a bitch!" he pleaded with all his soul.

The prisoner stared at him strangely.

"Untie me!" he said. "Untie me and let's fight! Let's see which of us survives."

Natividad sighed with relief. "Sounds like a good idea," he said to himself.

That would be different and honorable. To fight like two men, with no advantages, like sometimes in school when he was a boy, only now it would be to the death.

He untied the captain, who got up shrugging and stretching his arms.

"Very good!" he murmured.

But he had no intention of keeping his word. He immediately began to run away, zig-zagging between the cacti and maguey plants.

His running became steady and he appeared to be heading toward a nearby destination. Since he was very familiar with the region and since it had been his job as a spy for the *federales* to pay careful attention to it, he had plotted his escape for precisely when he knew himself to be near a federal campsite.

Oblivious to anything else, Natividad pursued him, and soon he himself became the pursued when the *federales* who were quartered in the nearby hills realized what was happening.

"Goddamned captain," said Natividad as he recalled the incident, and he moved his head while an indulgent, tranquil smile curved his lips. "What a dirty trick; for three days I walked around lost, unable to find the revolution."

The last phrase made an incredible impression in Adán's mind. "*Find the revolution!*" As if the revolution were a person, a woman, and she, tangible, physical, and defined, were being sought. He could say nothing about this revolution which was nothing more than total chaos and a bloody game. War was at best a way of seeking blood, of satisfying it, its only substance and objectives being perhaps those of releasing man's secret springs, his resentment, his extraordinary and astonishing barbarism, his total privation. In the revolution a man felt as if he were returning to discover himself, as if all the death, blood, and the freedom to transgress were its essence and program. Adán was therefore taken aback by the phrase that had suddenly assumed a certain profundity and a certain new value: "*Find the revolution!*" Go, take its hand, unite with it so intimately it would give birth to children, houses, land, heaven, the entire country. But Adán could not say a thing. *His* revolution was something else. It was the revolution engraved in his first impression, when, at the age of sixteen, he was serving under a certain general who was later executed.

The general, a very good marksman, was practicing one morning in the company of several officers. They were arguing about eighty steps away from the humble and simple gray adobe wall. A small coin served as the target in one of the holes in the wall.

One of the officers fired first, and then another. They were quite skillful marksmen, and their bullets landed only a few centimeters off-target. The general flashed a triumphant smile.

His body in profile, his arm slightly lifted, and his eyes aiming with absolute precision, his shot was like a straight line that extended from the barrel of his pistol to the very center of the coin. The coin fell admid a little puff of dust and the officers ran to pick it up. The general, strutting slowly and triumphantly, went to check the shot also. Nevertheless, its accuracy seemed in doubt.

"I don't think you hit it, my general," said one of the officers with the coin in his hand.

The general's cheeks and lips grew pale.

"That can't be," he exclaimed, barely containing his rage.

As if they were dealing with the most important matter in the world, they all leaned over and examined the coin. There was a shiny mark on the edge.

"Here it is!" said the general.

The officers moved their heads, faking astonishment.

"You're right, general. Congratulations."

But the general was not satisfied. He wanted an indisputable triumph that would be obvious from the first moment. He grew very nervous and frowned with rage.

Aware of what was going on, two of the officers went to place the coin back on the wall. One of them, the one who had first doubted the accuracy of the shot, stood a short distance away in order to verify the shot. He was a man of medium build and sharp eyes.

"Now, my general!" he shouted.

The general was not smiling. His stern face was slightly trembling and his eyes had suddenly become cold and unflinching. He moved an additional ten meters away and then, very slowly, raised the pistol up to the height of his shoulder. A movement as simple and as unhindered as this took on unexpectedly powerful force, decisiveness, and meaning. Everyone understood that the instant had become pregnant with solemnity and purpose, that it was a rare, solemn, and decisive moment. It was all just a matter of serenely taking aim, with nerves of steel and with absolute confidence. And then of squeezing the trigger. But this squeezing of the trigger was precisely what was so extraordinary, because this act always has its precise place in time and space, neither before nor after. And if that one second, that infinitesimal fraction of destiny that exists for it, passes, is lost and no longer exists, then everything has been in vain. All the links of the process leading up to that crucial second can be strung together with logic, objectivity, and coldness, but suddenly the point in time of the eye of the needle is reached, and that little eye becomes chance, luck, something far removed from the operation of human will and dominion.

The general lowered the pistol, without firing.

"No," he said, addressing the officer near the wall. "Better yet, I'll shoot you between your eyes, like I do lizards, I'm pretty good at that."

And he aimed again, this time between the officer's eyes.

The officer became ghostly pale but his lips were smiling: "Go ahead, my general!"

"No," answered the general, also smiling. But his smile announced that he was now feeling calm and composed. "Bring me one of last night's instead."

"Last night's" were three executed men whose bodies were clearly visible in the adjacent corral.

Adán had to bring one of these corpses, dragging it with great difficulty.

They propped the slumping corpse up between two adobe columns so it wouldn't fall over sideways.

The general took aim, uncontrollably laughing. His shot was so perfect that it made a tiny hole between the corpse's eyebrows just above the nasal bone, like a small mole.

The other shooters, less skillful, hit it in its forehead, jaws, and cheeks, which made the corpse fall forward, as if it had a stomachache. It began to look alive, as if it were participating in the game and wanted to play the clown.

"Now, you!" said the general, addressing Adán. "Let's see how good you are!"

Adán's shot was so far off that it barely grazed the corpse's head, leaving a white hairless part.

This was what Adán had to say about *his* revolution. Because his revolution was a fundamental, simple one of strange moods and a profound anxiety.

It was their racing aimlessly through mountains. It was their trampling over sowed fields. Yes, *precisely* their trampling over sowed fields. The furrows run parallel, with an intelligent, graceful symmetry. They run straight, obeying that profound discipline of the earth that demands uprightness, honor, and legitimacy. The endless extension of furrows re-sembles a net cast over the soil and throbbing life, ordering the growth. They obey a design, a material voice, which de-crees from underground the miracle of communion with the air, so that bread will come forth like a child, shoots of corn and wheat will find a home, and back-breaking toil will raise its glorious statue. But hatred also demands its own monu-ment, and trampling over a furrow becomes an act of invigo-rating negation. That is when man is unleashed like an ob-scure animal that finds its simple pleasure in desolation and chaos. His soul is possessed by a furious power and a subju-gating impurity which have been unleashed free and un-checked. Destruction raises its will and from then on there is nothing, because blindness embraces everything and there arises a senseless pleasure for the sowed fields and seed to burn to embers. That was the revolution: death and blood. Sterile blood and death; the luxury of fighting only for the subterranean doors of the soul to open wide permitting the tremendous, bestial solitude that man carries within him to be released in the form of an infinite, blood-curdling, and bitter shriek.

Adán stared at Natividad, trying to penetrate his inner-most breathing and destiny. In what revolution did Natividad believe? In what way did he believe? What new revolution did his words, his way of putting things, and his life convey? Where had they come from?

Adán became desperate when in contact with Natividad. He felt like a deaf man hearing a murmur, or something less than a murmur, or even something much less than the illusion of a murmur, and just about when he was on the verge of ac-tually hearing, something as slight and thin as a strand of hair imposed its definitive obstruction, making more dense the shadows of deafness, destroying all hope. Or he felt like a blind man on the verge of seeing, unable to cross the imponderable, fantastic line that exists between darkness and vision. Or like an insane man lacking the superhuman forces necessary to cross the frontier of one millionth of a millimeter that exists between reason and insanity.

It was impossible to understand Natividad's strong, hopeful world. From the very first moment, therefore, Adán felt a kind of superstitious fear, respect, and helpless impotence toward him.

It was a pleasant day and Adán and Natividad walked under its skies in a world of streams equidistant from all the water channels of the Irrigation System.

That was the first time Adán had had any dealing with Natividad and he remembered everything in detail: his voice, his eyes, his way of using words and tone in the right places.

Then came the second time, much later.

The third was somewhat different and Adán could not see anything in the darkness and only heard the sound of rapid, machine-gun fire which in just one moment consummated everything. "By treason." With Natividad it would be possible only by treason.

But there was something strange and unique in all of this that had never before taken place in Adán's soul. It was as if Natividad were powerful and multiple, made of hundreds of men and women and houses and wills.

The strike paralyzed the Irrigation System about six months after Natividad had arrived. In one instant everything was dead and the shirts, which were once clean on Saturday afternoons and all day Sunday, became ashen, grimy, while eyes sunk deep into the sockets of skulls like flames in a cave. The floodgates were all patrolled by groups of workers, and more than a hundred strikers guarded the dam.

One could not hear the slightest sound in the vast extension of the Irrigation System. Nevertheless, there was a movement, a marching. It was indeed a sound, the sound of steps that represented a kind of negation of all noise. Because a strike is what one finds on the edge of silence, but it is also silent itself. The strikers become silent, but they have a voice. They are standing still but it is as if they were walking. Men acquire another voice, another way of walking, and another look, and one begins to feel something powerful in the air rising like a firm mass. It is a question of absolute wonder. There is a substance nourished in the atmosphere, as if men's hearts had come together to erect walls of energy and as if something important and absolute were about to take place. Shoulders and backs feel a heavy weight upon them; pregnant hands acquire the absorbed and pensive quietude of young women about to become mothers, soon to be opened by the pure and original wail. It is a question of absolute wonder. Wonder and joy. One foot never walks alone; instead, it joins other feet which by the thousands can be heard in the voice, in the pulse, and in dreams during those long nights. One can hear the steps: during the clarity of noon, the steps; at sundown, at any hour, the steps; within the infinite encasement of time. The men, profoundly brought together around the red flag, are not moving. They are not moving, they are listening. There is a bell in the immensity of life that they are ringing, and they are reviving terrestrial and celestial layers so that it can be heard; but they are just standing there, mute, still, and in absolute silence under the flag.

A problem has been put before the assembly; it concerns the young son of one of the workers. He is sick, and suddenly this sickness moves the entire hall to trembling as if a corpulent, massive mother had extended her infinite arms. Sick. The strikers rise up one by one in the assembly and come up to the table to contribute their grimy, humble coins. The poorest of the poor also puts his tiny tribute there. He had run to his house in an instant and still panting had left a homely, broken doll under the president's hands for the sick child. There the doll lies with its blood of sawdust.

The assembly responds so well to the responsibilities of solidarity that one of the workers feels obligated to rise and go up to the platform:

"Enough, *compañeros*," he says; his voice is heard full of dignity and pride despite his tattered, soiled clothing. "We are not a mutual aid society; we are a revolutionary trade union."

Then he shouts:

"We don't want the happiness of just one child but the happiness and health of all the children of the world."

The enthusiastic uproar of the response drowns out his last words. He has uttered nonsense. The strike is simply seeking a wage increase and the reduction of the work day. After the strike poor children will continue to be sick and sad and poor. But how powerful, extraordinary, and wonderful is this nonsense! His words are immaculate and pure, and the truth that they contain could not be greater. It is the steps. Here is the red flag which will soon fade with the sun and air, becoming as humble and tattered as the men it shelters. But listen to the noise. No, it is not noise. It is a form of silence, the form steps take when men march behind hope.

Fifteen days later, some forty Indians appeared, wretched and completely drunk. They had first been offered tequila and mescal, but they had refused it, preferring pure alcohol instead. The large cups of alcohol had stabbed them with dizzying accuracy and the Indians became meek, incomprehensible, and sad immediately after the first blow, looking with humble, tender gratefulness at the strikebreaker recruiter who had given them the alcohol. The recruiter pretended to be making sure that they did not go too far, but that was precisely all part of his plans. The Indians looked suspiciously at how they filled the first cup, and they simply smiled timidly, adopting the attitude of those who do not feel deserving of kindness or affection. Later, after they had drunk the alcohol and were still grimacing because of its savageness, their laughter became franker and bolder and their eyes glistened with a small spark. Another cup. As the alcohol penetrated, they became saddened and furious at the same time. It was their suffering and their rage. Suddenly they became aware of their sorrows; and their terrifying impotence before their weary, obscure, and ancient past inexplicably moistened their eyes with gratitude, submission, and supplication. One more cup.

"That's the last one," said the scab recruiter. "If not, you'll all be drunk."

But he prepared a drink of alcohol for each one anyway. They would drink it later.

The Indians were moving their arms as if fighting off invisible spider webs. Something was bothering them and they could not understand a single word of the speaker, who was urging them to leave the farm guarded by the strikers.

Dazed and stubborn, they refused to leave. By now they were feeling an unexpected and distorted hatred, because they were remembering things, all the indignities and insults, and their entire lifeless, faithless lives.

The speaker was waving his arms, and he repeated:

"Haven't they taken away your land? The land of your fathers and grandfathers? Aren't you their victims also?"

But the alcohol was too insurmountable an obstacle. Though they were not actively belligerent, the Indians experienced a certain obstinance and impunity, as if they had been given back something, chaos perhaps, or certain obscure rights of vengeance and retaliation; in any case they did not yet dare to take up the new road. They were free now, but free from what? Free, now they could drink their bottle of alcohol without stopping and pass out dead drunk. Like animals, they could desire their neighbor's wife and curse whomever they pleased without having to stop drinking, drinking with all their souls, until they began to bleed.

They began to feel alone and confused about what was happening. A general mental withdrawal had already numbed them, except for three or four stubborn men who continued to look resentfully at the speaker.

One of the oldest of these went up to him:

"We want to work with these hands," he said, holding out his open hands, "but you won't let us."

The speaker stopped cold; his eyes were still flashing from his efforts to convince the hardened, savage mass of Indians.

"And how much are they going to pay you?"

The three or four Indians who had suddenly developed a vague and somewhat dull interest in the problem surrounded the speaker, squeezing in on him.

"They're going to pay us *pesos*," replied the old man, bragging, staggering from side to side.

This dialogue could clearly be used to arouse the scabs, so the speaker raised his voice so everyone could hear him.

"How many *pesos*?"

The old Indian did not know how many. He turned his curious eyes toward the recruiter.

"How many *pesos, compañero*?"

Caught and compromised by the question, the recruiter gave back an apprehensive look.

"They're not *pesos*," he said smiling. "*Centavos*, fifty *centavos*."

The mass of Indians was understanding everything with great difficulty. The alcohol circulated in their veins obfuscating all logic, only exciting in them the desire to drink even more.

In a leap, the speaker went right up to the scab recruiter, a plump, timid, and fat-cheeked little man. He grabbed him by the collar and punched him squarely in the face. When the recruiter hit the ground, he flung himself on top of him, wrenched his pistol away from him, and kicked him toward a small hill.

"Tell them," he ordered, "that you have tricked them and were going to rob them."

Lowering his head, the recruiter said:

"I wanted to get you drunk so I could get your money."

The four Indians looked at one another and the same old man climbed up the hill.

"*Compañeros, señores* strikers," he exclaimed in Spanish, and then in his own language he began to address the other Indians. Because of the effect of his drunkenness, his speech was long and perhaps excessively digressive because he gesticulated a lot, moaned at times, and became incredibly agitated. One could make out Spanish words—*virgen, centavos, Dios, huelga, señor*—interspersed among his words like islands, and then he turned around.

"We're going to kill you, old man," he said simply, addressing the recruiter.

The Indians whistled their approval. The repulsive, potbellied recruiter's jaws lowered, and his face turned pathetically ashen. He tried to kneel down, but they began beating him.

The strikers tried to intervene:

"A beating will be enough."

But it was impossible to contain the drunks who had already brutally and awkwardly subdued the man.

They dragged him searching for a tree from which to hang him.

"Just a beating," pleaded the workers.

The old Indian lifted his arm with his elbow pointing ahead, as if he were leaning on a window in another dimension.

"We're going to kill him. And that's that."

The crowd of a hundred men, counting both strikers and Indians, moved aimlessly, some enraged, others absolutely calm, and still others in despair.

"Don't kill him!"

In a manner of speaking, the recruiter was already dead. Dazed by the blows, the events seemed totally alien to him, totally unrelated to his person, referring instead to some other corporal, living, thinking individual dressed in his own flesh accompanying him, inside of him, among his murderers.

Faces, fists, voices, eyes, teeth, heads, words, arms, jaws, chins, screams, chests, that was the multitude. Silence, rage, bitterness, desire, fury, resentment, justice, breathing, physiology. A human sea. Men made of wave after wave of rocks, fish, and monsters. Staring faces resembling scales, gigantic scales, mixed with the air, the round, spherical air of stone, scales with saliva, knives, in the muddy air.

"Don't kill him!"

He was not in the slightest pain; he was numb, looking down at the multitude as if he were suspended over violent, dry, and raging water.

"What do you mean, don't kill him?"

Under the tree, the body was practically a sack, whose moving contents were intestines and lungs, among other things. It was difficult to hoist him up because the tree was so small, and the man remained on his knees with a slack in the rope. The stones continued raining down on him and his death was guaranteed, but not by hanging since the small tree was simply inadequate.

As a matter of fact, he did not die until night came, and then probably only of thirst, well after all the Indians and strikers had disappeared, which was sometime before noon.

He had been left alone terrified with a rope around his neck for many hours, and he had uttered a slight noise like that of a bumblebee inside a pumpkin blossom. Later, at about nine-thirty or eleven o'clock, the noise uneventfully stopped. He died of thirst, probably only of thirst.

The authorities scoured the entire System with their investigations. They had learned that the old Indian's name was Chuy and they wanted to find him, but Chuy was already back in the mountains.

The three Indians who were apprehended five days later said nothing and remembered nothing. When the authorities arrested them they were still drunk. It was said that they were going to shoot them in a contrived escape attempt.

At that time, with the strike strengthened by workers from other units, the entire Irrigation System grew silent under the omnipotent force of five thousand strikers.

The committee was forced to order the floodgates and canals of the dam closed so that the water would not be wasted.

The creative, redemptive water.

Many years before, the System had been an uninhabited, solitary wasteland. The land, most of it useless limestone, had belonged to an extensive *latifundio*. When the revolution was twenty or twenty-two years old, it finally became interested in these lands. It would construct its masterwork on them.

Next to the river, there was a small village with a church. A wretchedly miserable village. It is difficult to explain how the inhabitants of such a village live, eating only roots. The black, dark houses were made of wood or tin, which made their inhabitants look the same color.

At dawn, the men would begin to march like ghosts toward the mountains more than fifty kilometers away. Actually, it was before dawn, while it was still completely dark, and they were not exactly ghosts, but, rather, voices and steps, which the women, inside amid the crying of their children, were able to identify unerringly, recognizing in them their husbands, oldest sons, and brothers. The men would march without incident toward the mountain, returning in the late afternoons with piles of firewood, a dead deer or some twenty trout from far up the river. They managed, nevertheless; they managed to live. Precisely *what* they lived on is beside the point. It may be true that thick, black *tortillas* made of course cornmeal with chile and salt do not actually nourish, but they do help keep the soul alive, maintaining itself like a climbing *huizache* vine shaken by the wind. That's what these hundred, two hundred, inhabitants of the village were: *huizache* vines covered with dust that had become very small and could hardly utter a brief moan amid their drooping branches.

In any case, the river was a god. Evil river, evil god, with the languid, sickly water of the yearly rainfall. The villages would then gather around it, offering up their thanks for the river, for their crumbs of daily bread.

But one day, engineers, bricklayers, mechanics, and painters began to arrive and set up shop, and the wretched village suddenly flourished. The boom lasted for some time, but then came the strike, the defeat, and finally the exodus.

The strike: five thousand silent men, hardened by faith. They were not together in outward appearance, but they could be felt in the atmosphere, like an additional weight, like an infinite muscle, surrounding and then invading the silent extension of land. The committees stationed themselves at each one of the floodgates, and during the closing of the main floodgate they held a kind of ceremony, with speeches.

What had once been a limestone wilderness had become, when the System was functioning smoothly and the dam wall had not yet begun to crack, a landscape resonant with masculine vigor, where men were bent in labor.

That same afternoon after his second meeting with Natividad and his having run into the group of strikers, Adán roamed the plain, depressed and somber. The afternoon twilight was like a drab mare stomping over the same spot before taking off. It stomped in place on the very edge of the horizon, one, two, three, four, five, six times, like an impatient gray mare being held back right before a competition, unable to transform itself from a mare or centaur of clouds into something else, until suddenly darkness comes, a horse or a large bird, like a wall, an impenetrable drop curtain from the farthest sky to the deepest earth.

It was written that Natividad would die. It was written that it would be that night. It was written that his wife Cecilia—and later his widow and Ursulo's wife—would fall apart, running like a madwoman, her head engulfed in darkness.

Adán had shaken Natividad's hand when they parted at kilometer 25 after their first meeting. Adan's memory insisted that from the very first moment it had been a full, deeply friendly hand. All this was written, however Adán at first could not believe that fate had such a precise, definite, and irrefutable existence. Nevertheless, Natividad would be shot to death, crucified. And where was Cecilia running to with her hair flying in the wind? Where was the madwoman running? But for some reason, this was the way it had to be. This was the way. In life, in the night, in that particular night.

"Unless by treachery." And why not by treachery?

Adán roamed the night plotting that death. Magnificent shadows engulfed him as he walked, as if he were walking in space. And precisely there in the darkness he would commit the murder. In two hours perhaps. In the far distance he could see Natividad's house, from which the yellow light of petroleum was filtering out. The two shadows, Cecilia and Natividad, were moving, and the house vibrated with the healthy laughter of people absolutely alive. "The time has come. He's home," he said to himself, and he went in search of his accomplices.

When he arrived at his own house, he was met with La Borrada's breathing in the otherwise unlit doorway where she had been waiting for him.

"Is that you?" Adán asked fearfully.

"Yes," replied the solemn voice.

Adán was overcome with fear and might have wanted to beat her and protest in some way, but it would have been extremely terrifying to refuse to submit to this powerful, invisible female. He did just the opposite. Disoriented, abandoned, and totally alone in the world, he kneeled before her and begged for forgiveness. It was fear. Infinite fear.

"Don't light the candle," he begged. "Don't light it."

And he was about to add "please," but he checked himself.

They entered the shack.

There he lost her.

"Borrada! Where are you?"

The tangible breathing—it was right beside him, on his face—replied:

"Here!" And it was an unreal breathing, from another world, possessing volume in the darkness.

"Don't light it," Adán repeated, because he was savagely frightened that his plans might be discovered even by her.

"Look," he began, but La Borrada interrupted him. She-wolf. Loving beast.

"You don't need to tell me," she said with incredible clarity. "You're going to kill Natividad."

"Yes," whispered Adán, and he trembled, actually kneeling, his teeth chattering.

"Don't kill him." But this time she appeared very far away and without breath.

"Borrada! Borrada!"

"Don't kill him."

Her voice came from very far away, from regions of the past. Adán began to search for her, groping through the shack. She could see in the darkness, like a goddess, and she could be anywhere, in any part of the world. "Borrada! Borrada!"

"Here I am!" and he again felt the breathing on his forehead.

"Why did you go away?"

"No, I haven't moved."

Was she lying? In any case, she was mistress now. He was in her kingdom.

Adán looked for the matches in every corner of his clothing, in his shirt, in his pants. A century later, he made a small light.

There was the woman. But she was not the woman of the instant before, the one with the breathing, the beast, the she-wolf. Bent over herself, she was sobbing in utter misery, her green eyes glistening with tears.

"Look," Adán began again, making a tremendous effort to overcome his weakness. "Go look for those two guys. Tell them to bring their horses. Tell them that they already know what for."

La Borrada suddenly raised her eyes, now cold and no longer tearful.

"I'll go," she said.

What is the wind and where does it begin, from what precise corner? All of a sudden it blows over the earth; it invades the planet; it sobs endlessly over the profound violin of midday. Its sobbing over the earth weeps for man's chains, chains felt more profoundly when the word of the wind races through the world. I am here, parched plant, dark branch, and outside is the wind. Sword, brother, furious flower, free me from this prison, liberate me. You are the slow horse pacing around in the garden among the bleeding roses, as if in a circus, and you are the hunter, the horn and the pack of hounds behind the clouds. But you are also the planet and damnation, the only solitude of man. Where is your cave? Where is the poisonous infinite tear of which you are made? The wind passes once, once again, and again, a thousand times. It passes. Both men and ages disappear over the earth. But the wind remains.

They draped flags over Natividad's corpse. An impressive crowd carried him to the cemetery in the atrium of the village church.

It was a miserable village, but during the boom period of the System it also had its happy period. That was when they sold all sorts of goods, fabrics, drinking alcohol, and hardware. On Sundays the market was like a fiesta of colors, buzzing with calico, blankets, dyes, and leather. The little village had its ups and downs, until the final disaster, when there was no other choice and everyone was forced to emigrate, to flee, in search of other land. Only the silent, hermetic priest remained in the church, dying of hunger and abandoned by his flock.

The periods of prosperity or misfortune were always determined by the river.

An old man looking at it liked to exclaim:

"It is our mother and our father. Sometimes it gives us and sometimes it denies us. We will die in its hands."

Muddy river; its water was never clear. That explained the ash-colored bodies and the soiled clothing.

Nevertheless it was a small blessing when the discolored waters were flowing. But suddenly, it was as if a hand, a gigantic hand, had intervened from above, permitting only a filthy trickle, thick like saliva, to reach the land. And you could see it in the women's hopeless and suffering faces. If they could have cried, their tears would have been enough to form a strong, deep current in the bed of the dry river. But no.

It could be seen in their faces, without having to go to the river to confirm it and observe how raw sewage, the incredible stomach of a dead dog, and fetid mud were piling up in the river bed.

Then, as if fate were toying with them, once again the swollen, thundering river returned.

Because they were unfamiliar with happiness, the only visible sign on their faces was a certain brilliance in their stares. One could also actually tell that there was water in the river simply by looking into their eyes, simply by observing how the ashes of their lips were beginning to dissolve.

Then came those two or three years of prosperity and happiness. A dam was built upstream.

Engineers, contractors, brick-layers, mechanics, and carpenters populated everything with an intense, vital sound, as if it were not a dam but a statue, not any less beautiful than a statue, that they were sculpting to adorn the gray landscape. Two or three years. Maybe four or five, counting the time it took to construct the dam. A happiness charged with vigor, the buzzing of trucks loaded with cement, the precise language of hammers. New men were being born, with new faces, new hands, new voices. The ancient, ancestral peasant who today drove a cement mixer, in firm, close contact with that brand-new, graceful material, was like a young god in virile overalls. He was building the statue; he was raising that music of steel, sand, wood, and gravel over the earth, condensing the air little by little to turn it into the statue, first the feet and the dark skeleton, then the entire body with its curtains and vestiture, like an ancient majestic and solemn amphitheater.

The cursed, erratic river was made a prisoner. Its waters were enclosed, and even calculating that same fickleness in the rains, the engineers claimed that the reservoir had a capacity for five years of irrigation.

186

They did not, of course, count on the cracks in the cement wall.

Later came the exodus. Everyone fled and the System's lands returned to their former state, when they were simply parts of a desperate and irredeemable wasteland.

The impoverished little village beside the river also fled. Only the sad and watchful priest, abandoned inside his small church without his parish, remained.

Insidious, cunning river, triumphant in the end! Men were helpless before its stubborn will, its waters and its whims, cursed river.

Before the System was established, there was nevertheless in the village what could be called a certain "life." In the evenings shadows would move up and down the streets and strange individuals would meet with the priest in the church. Something mysterious was developing, as if announcing that the grave and sinister acts occurring in the rest of the country would reach even this small corner of Mexico.

On the church vestibule's notice board, on which they put up daily religious announcements, today was an angry message, written in black letters, with a black cross under which could be read the name of the Bishop of Huejutla. It had to do with the famous "Third Message to the Civilized World," in which the bold bishop was calling for open rebellion.

No one in the village knew the Bishop of Huejutla, not even where Huejutla was located. Where? Some emphatically insisted that it was in Sonora, others in Chiapas, and there was even someone who said that it was in Yucatán.

"*Señor* Calles is arousing all levels of government to go to whatever lengths necessary, because our children and youth must belong to the revolution," said the message.

The troops of Jesus were not especially numerous in the region, but they were unusually cold-blooded, unusually furious, bold, terrifying, and fanatic. They were neither cowardly nor brave; they were simply blind, a millenary force, with silex in their guts.

On one occasion, they brought back with them a young rural schoolteacher and cut out his tongue in the outskirts of the village. The young man looked as if he had been drinking blood by the bucketful.

"Don't you want a little mescal," Guadalupe, the Cristero chief, asked him, "to refresh yourself?"

What could the teacher answer? Just some guttural and stomach sounds, but definitely not articulated in his mouth.

"Let's do it!" and the Cristero chief was smiling.

They brought the teacher a full cup and forced his clenched teeth open with a machete so he would drink the burning fire with his bloody, tongueless mouth.

"Come on! Let's see you shout right now what you were shouting earlier," continued the Cristero. "What was it? *Viva la revolución*? We'll give you your revolution!"

"Will you permit, oh fathers, your sons to be victims of the revolution?" continued the Bishop of Huejutla. "Will you permit the sons of your flesh to be devoured by the infernal animal pack that has dug its claws into the breast of the fatherland?"

Miracles took place also, and they were passed on from mouth to mouth, like the one about the cross.

There was once a confrontation with some federal troops half a kilometer from the village. The *federales* certainly believed in God, in Christ, and in the Church. So it made no sense that they were fighting with such rage and hatred. The confrontation took place in the Mexican countryside; that is to say, as if bloodless and unreal, far off in the moderate, discreet lands of El Bajío. Small churches dot the rectangles of the villages and fields. Nothing can possibly happen there, yet two groups of men are attacking each other:

one dressed in white, with large hats and cotton pants; another in olive green, with army caps and leggings. They attack as if without hatred, but death is clearly present as is, of course, a profound boiling anger.

A Cristero soldier had been horribly wounded. His head had been blown to bits leaving only his grotesque, savage trunk. It may seem fantastic or incredible, but the headless, drunk Cristero got up, zig-zagged and stumbled backward and finally fell at the foot of the cross that stood at the entrance to the village. No one wiped off the blood from that cross which they say began to grow like a tree, as if the blood were the necessary water, the indispensable yeast.

Could anyone actually doubt the existence of God? Merciful God who erases the sins of the world?

"Will you even tolerate," thundered the frothful words of that frenetic Savonarola of Huejutla, "will you tolerate the Bolshevik monster first penetrating the sanctuary of your descendants in order to destroy the religion of your forefathers and then raising the flag of the devil?"

A terrifying river came into being cutting the entire country in two. It was a dirty river, full of blood, with blind eyes and clenched teeth.

"And will we go, we, the true Mexicans, the young men of the Catholic Church, the victors of so many and such glorious battles, the cherished children of Christ the King?"

The word had been spoken. Jesus had been crowned, and in his hands was placed the furious tiara of a king. King, king, king of the Jews. Christ, *Cristo Rey*, Christ the King.

"*Viva Cristo Rey!*"

Cristo Rey reached every corner of Mexico, and he could be seen in houses, rooms, communities, in the wretched artesan shops, either as the Sacred Heart of Jesus, red and bloody, with flames in his chest and a wound in the middle of the ventricles of his burning viscera, or as the Christ of Venom, blackened, full of smoke, wood without light, or even in the form of the insane statues, with sores on his knees, blood on his lips, and a lost look on his face.

The revolution, for its part, one might say, was waged for a Church. This was a much more tragically confusing period than others. The mediocre and fanatic patriarch Perez, a Catholic priest, promoted the schism.

He advocated the creation of a Catholic Church far away from the Roman authority of the Sovereign Pontiff, a national Church "in accordance with the law."

The peasants did not understand the difference between these two Churches when they were actually inside a church kneeling before a priest who celebrated mass in the same way, with the same ceremonies and rituals as the traditional Church. Indeed, the two Churches had come into being based on the very same obscure, subterranean, disoriented, and tormented sentiment, a sentiment that beat in a people lacking religion in the strict, pragmatic sense of the word, but nevertheless a religious, fervent, devout people, more in search of divinity, their own divinity, than already in possession of it; they had no gods. The Spaniards blundered when they destroyed the pagan temples in order to construct Catholic ones in their place. This policy never actually resulted in the extinction of one religion so another could replace it, but, rather, in the extinction of all religion and all religious feeling. The Spanish Colony rapidly came into being through fraud—perhaps following the example of the casuistic and careless Christopher Columbus—and was able with relative ease *to fool* the high dignitaries of the Church, both in Rome as well as on the peninsula, by means of exaggerated reports regarding the "conversion" of the infidels. The theological jurists of the Colony cared more for the canon than they did for souls, and if the letter of the law were respected the Indians would be allowed to remain fundamentally idolaters.

190

Something began to be lacking in the people ever since: land, god, Tlaloc, Christ; yes, land. What could they ever hope for?

The same men who had built the solid, incomprehensible, barbaric, and perhaps bloody temples, or *teocalis*, were later to capture the wonder of the unsurpassed, linear, profound Catholic temples. But in whatever temple one looked, in Tlatelolco, in Puebla, or in Oaxaca, he would see climbing with ecstatic slowness amid its stones a serpent, eyes sad with nostalgia, leaving its question behind, that impossible look that asks itself where and in what place.

A revolution with a Church, priests, and absurd Christs. Blood began to flow above the despair of the people and they began to fight senselessly and desperately, for no other reason than to end it all and die. The cross was growing. The cross of the miracle, drenched in blood, like a plant, a monstrous growing cross, the cross of the headless *Cristero*.

It was all so incredible, so senseless and insane: the useless blood, the ferocity, the hatred, the filthy river black with saliva in the middle of the country, the creeping serpent, what did it all mean? What was the mystery? Who were these amazing, terrifying people? These questions could only be answered by the radical and definitive dispossession man had been forced to endure, and if he therefore defended God it was because in God he was defending the vague, trembling, terrifying notion of feeling himself master of something, master of God, master of the Church, master of stones, of what he had never possessed: land, truth, light, or who knows what other magnificent, powerful thing.

In the small village, life suddenly began to pull itself up onto its own feet, but it did so carelessly and brutally, as if a sick man had been given an overdose of some active heart stimulant, tossing and turning over himself not knowing what to do with his hands, which were jumping like springs, nor with his eyes, which could see through stone. No one had understood the words of either the Bishop of Huejutla or the apostolic delegate, words that were circulating throughout the entire country, words which, on the other hand, had never been written to be understood. But everyone, men, women, and children, rose up at the call of an elementary voice, the roots of whose sound did not even have a name.

They fortified the church with weapons brought in from who knows where, perhaps by other Cristero groups.

Guadalupe, chief of the rebels, was meeting with the priest:

"Let's see if they'll come," he said, referring to the *federales*. "Let's see if they dare, those bastards," he fumed with dry rage.

Nevertheless, the next day, when bands of *federales* and *agraristas* arrived, Guadalupe had to surrender and allow another priest, the schismatic priest, to take over the church.

After the village had been pacified, Adán, who was with the *federales,* rode through the main streets accompanied by twenty men, dragging women out of their houses in order for them to tell where their husbands were hiding, but he was not given the slightest information.

He then returned to the church, where the prisoners were being held: Guadalupe, Valentín and several others.

He led them to the back of the church.

"Sons of bitches!" he muttered as he fired at Guadalupe.

Valentín, perhaps suddenly seized by an attack of insanity as he watched his companion fall, began to run, in vain, as it turned out, because one second later one of Adán's bullets wounded him in the left foot. "What rotten luck," he thought.

"You were trying to escape, weren't you, you jerk?" Adán said, joking with infinite cruelty. "Come on. Let's go to the town hall so you can get what you deserve."

He did not take him to the town hall or anywhere else. They both passed through the town until a little after noon, as if strolling along serenading, Adán on horseback and the Cristero behind him, limping because of his wound.

At twelve-thirty or perhaps at one o'clock—the church clock had died a long time ago—perhaps even at two o'clock, it looked as if the pair were actually heading toward the town hall. But this was not true.

They aimlessly roamed the inclement earth, among the cacti. They would never go anywhere.

Adán continued on horseback and Valentín staggered behind him, his foot swollen and green, dragged by a rope. They continued this way for several hours.

Finally, Valentín collapsed in the dust:

"I'm not walking!" he coughed, instead of actually speaking.

There were no longer degrees of suffering; walking and refusing to go on were now the same thing. In his foot the formation of planets and a shrill, spinning solar system was taking place.

Adán smiled, powerful master of pain and life. His spurs sunken into his horse's flanks represented in their cruel and serrated circumference the space and time of pain. One single turn, as in the wheel of fate, and the suffering would intensify unimaginably. He decided to sink them deep into the beast's flesh, and it took off in a gallop.

Valentín, his distorted body now in the shape of a fat knot, was still being dragged along the ground, and he was complaining as weakly as a sleeping, sickly child. Then Adán stopped his horse.

"No," he said. "It's no fun this way." And he dismounted and lifted up the Cristero.

Grabbing him under his arms, he made him sit up.

"Let's go!" he appealed to him with false compassion. "Don't you see that we have to get to the town hall?"

Some superhuman spring must have burst in Valentín's soul, because suddenly with a strength that came from deep within him, he spat in Adán's face.

Adán turned pale.

"Don't be a fool. I don't want to kill you," he said with the same compassionate tone. "Come on, we have to get to the town hall."

The Cristero's eyes opened wide. He was smiling. No. He was not smiling. Perhaps he was going crazy.

"Why don't you say anything?" continued Adán, as if talking to a stubborn child. "Why are you just sitting there? Say something! Let's go!"

Valentín's eyes grew even wider.

"I want to die."

Adán, who had been squatting while he spoke with the Cristero, got up and headed for his horse.

"All right. If that's what you want. What can we do?"

He dragged him a considerable distance to the trunk of a gigantic cactus. He tied him to it tightly.

Thick drops ran down Valentín's forehead.

"What? You're not going to kill me?"

Adán burst out laughing.

"No. I'm leaving you here. It's better to let the buzzards eat you."

He then slowly rode away and found a shrub behind which he could observe Valentín without his noticing and enjoy himself at his expense.

The Cristero tried to shout but he was too weak and simply whimpered.

This went on for a half-hour. During that century Adán had smoked maybe five cigarettes.

Then, without making a sound—it is absolutely certain, nevertheless, that Valentín felt those steps—Adán drew near, the pistol in his hand.

"Get moving!" he said, one second before firing.

The Cristero must have felt the steps and even anticipated the shot, because when Adán approached him from the front to look at him, he attempted a signal with his index finger thrust straight up, as if saying: "Another one, just one more and that'll be it." One more bullet.

The priest had fled the village just before it fell to the *federales* and *agraristas*. However, from some hiding point he was able to observe the death of Guadalupe whom Adán had shot against the back wall of the church. He therefore fled absolutely terrorized, the terror of death circulating in his veins. He had always been afraid to die, enormously afraid. He felt that death was like a special, exaggerated life of consciousness, a life in which only consciousness, free of physical, social, and terrestrial limitations, acted to strip man's spirit, penetrating it like nothing had ever penetrated it before. That was when the horror would occur, an inhuman horror, beyond anything we know, where a never-sleeping consciousness one by one discovered corners which in the moments before death it had always denied, but which afterward could not be contradicted.

A few days later, the peasants of the village went in search of the priest to tell him what had happened. They sat down around a crooked table and the priest listened to their simple sentences which nevertheless contained so much truth and life.

"With all due respects, *padre,*" they were saying, "but the bastard forced him to walk through the town with his wounded foot."

"And his foot was already turning purple."

They told him about Valentín's sacrifice, and the polite-ness of their expressions, "With all due respects" and "with-out intending to offend anyone here," revealed their cautious, discreet, and modest sense of things.

The priest listened covering his face with his hands so the peasants would not discover his warring emotions, his fear and his solitude.

Valentín's death was not different from the death of the young school teacher whose tongue the Cristeros had cut out before forcing him to drink mescal. There was equal hatred on both sides, an equal savage impulse for torture.

The priest was thinking about this, recalling the minutes before the sacrifice of the young teacher. Guadalupe and Valentín—the same ones Adán was to murder—had come to consult with him.

"We're going to shoot him, *padre*," they said.

As a priest, perhaps he could have prevented it. But a pa-thetic impotence had atrophied his will. He did not utter a single word. Perhaps he could have asked them to do it with-out any cruelty, but he found it impossible to formulate even this demand. Why? He had contributed to unleashing forces that were superior to himself, forces of rage and of an atro-cious faith that dominated everything. He was incapable of dominating the violence.

He asked himself therefore if truth was not to be found on either side and if all that tragic confusion was nothing more than the discovery of the uncharted abyss and cesspool of men. Could one believe in anything? Why was everything unjust? What would become of the village? Where was its his-tory? Hatred. Hatred. Hatred. Hatred. Hatred. Hatred. Fifty kinds of hatred. Sanctified hatred and other kinds. But he knew that this was not the problem. He felt a terrifying fear: he was going to die without knowing the truth, and his body, his eyes, his hands, his entire being, would become pure consciousness, the consciousness of consciousness, abstract and chemically pure consciousness, sleepless or incomprehensibly clear-sighted consciousness. The country needed something else, but who knew what?

"Let's go!" he told the peasants.

"Where to, *padre?*"

"I mean, forgive me," he corrected himself. "I'm going alone. Let me go alone."

He walked barefoot for several hours, cutting his feet on the stones, until he reached the spot where Valentín had died. All that remained was the rope and a little black blood on the gigantic trunk of the cactus.

Why those shadows hovering over and obstructing man's intelligence? And so it happened that Valentín—a gloomy, fanatical criminal—had become a martyr, and a martyr of religion. The inhabitants of the village risked their lives, hiding from the federal troops, by making secret pilgrimages to that cactus, that monstrous, authentic Mexican cross, to pray beneath the plant's three or four sinister arms.

The priest found three women there, as if actually reenacting a Biblical passage. Valentín, victim of fury, a martyr, a Christ! He felt infinite shame and a desire to weep. A Christ, Christ the King.

"Get out of here! Go away!" he shouted.

The women ran away frightened and then the priest sat down on a rock, his head in his hands, and began to weep. He too had no Church; he too had no faith. Nor did he have God.

Natividad descended into his grave burning with banners, aflame, surrounded by the silent, utterly silent multitude. That was when the town was beginning to decay, three months into the strike, and hunger began to harden their faces.

Before, when everything was peaceful, one could clearly hear the murmur of the percale being measured with a wooden yardstick in the plaza. A murmur of paper, of hearth, wife, and clean home. But when Natividad died, that sound had not been heard for some time.

The faces were different now, as if immersed in a pool of reflections. Natividad being lowered into the earth wrapped in red banners. He was descending.

The piercing scream of a woman was heard but no one bothered to turn his head. What for?

It was La Borrada in the crowd. She had suddenly understood something so clearly and mercilessly, and she covered her face and ran like a madwoman in search of Adán.

Back home, they stared at each other as if in shock.

An ugly, copper-colored piece of dried beef hung from the ceiling.

La Borrada experienced a sudden hatred for that meat that looked so human.

"Are they coming?" Adán asked, terrified.

La Borrada's green eyes instilled fear.

Something unexplainable, a furious desire for salvation, an awesome repentance, made her cry out:

"Let's get out of here!"

Adán did not know what to say.

"Are they coming? Are they coming?" he repeated, despite La Borrada's indications that they were not.

"Let's get out of here!"

The cursed dried beef hanging there from the ceiling, with four bloated motionless flies.

"This death is different," said La Borrada. Adán grabbed her by the shoulders.

"What do you mean?"

Adán's hands were wet with the woman's tears.

"It's different," she repeated.

It was strange that for someone so withdrawn, so silent, and so astonishingly solemn in her exterior manifestations she would today, with her eyes the color of the moon, the color of a lake, shed such intense, green, and beloved tears. That she would today reveal a certain profound bond, a certain community of blood. "So she loves me," Adán thought, as if a knife of light had torn open his soul. "She loves me." He had never bothered to confirm this, and now his first impression was as if they had extracted some of his blood, weakening him sweetly and incredibly. For the first time in his life he felt tenderness, happiness, a totally confident resignation. "Is it true that I love her too?" he asked himself, and just when he understood that he indeed did love her, he realized that everything had ended for him, that from that moment on he would begin to pay for his sins and would begin to be alone, alone with her, pursued relentlessly for centuries, like Cain. He was unarmed. It was good.

Sad for the first time in his life, he asked again:

"What do you mean?"

She was absolutely open and transparent, but she could not express her thoughts:

"It is not a death like the others," she said. "Today you didn't wound just one man."

Adán understood. He had understood for some time. He understood ever since the day he was commissioned with Natividad's death, because he had perceived what that man full of youth, new strength, and mysterious power represented. Men like Natividad would rise up one morning throughout the land of Mexico; it would be a sunny morning. New men, and smiling. And no one would be able to stop these new men because they would represent enthusiasm and genuine emotion.

"Let's go, yes!" said Adán, superstitious, convinced of his own agony.

They fled from the crowd to hide from its stares.

The crowd is a negative sum of men; it never manages to take on a superior consciousness. It is animal, but like animals themselves, it is pure, perhaps better, worse also, than man himself.

The crowd is the chorus, fate, the obstinate chant.

One might ask where it ends, because it has no end.

For example, I myself might ask where my own limits begin, distinguishing me from the chorus, and where the border lies between my own blood and the other immense blood of mankind, the two bloods that form me.

I am the counterpoint, the analogous and opposite entity. The multitude surrounds me in my solitude, in my refuge, the pure multitude, war, the multitude of Mexico hoarse with hidden tears, the profound, inflamed Soviet multitude that surrounded Stalin, that surrounds me, that surrounds you.

A relentless eye was established to pursue Cain. And Cain saw it everywhere, but especially in his solitude. The eye, the chorus, destiny, the multitude, history.

"You didn't see them," La Borrada said. "They were terrifying when they were burying Natividad. You shouldn't have killed him."

But there was nothing he could do. Natividad went down into his grave, as if they had buried a hearthfire. The earth received him in order to join its flames to the internal fire that it fueled in his heart.

What was Natividad? What was the multitude? What were the masses?

Natividad was a child of the masses; in them he nourished his tremendous faith. The masses divided up the bread of history and with this bread Natividad was fed. How could he ever die? Just like in the ancient Egyptian rituals, the masses gave food, daily bread, to the living dead. It was a secret and new bread, nutritious, immortal, immortalizing.

"It's as if I hadn't killed him," thought Adán. "And now they want me to kill Ursulo, when he too is beyond death."

"Those men," added La Borrada, "have spirits that protect them. Birds and snakes and other guardians."

When they proposed that Adán kill Ursulo, the new leader of the strikers, Adán had accepted, feeling strong again, even if for only a few seconds, and willing to tempt his obscure destiny once more. Nevertheless, La Borrada was right there, a kind of conscience, a kind of covenant.

On that occasion, after Adán had slapped her, the woman, her lips bloodied, remained crouched in her corner, mute and motionless, eternal conscience and profound covenant.

Adán stood in the doorway, with his back to her, looking grimly into the distance where the envoy was slowly disappearing.

He now understood that he was beaten. That slap to La Borrada's face was simply a way to affirm his ebbing power. It was simply a demonstration of his impotence.

"I'm not the same," he said to himself, coming back into his house.

They remained opposite each other for several hours, without speaking. Finally, Adán spoke about the tragic assignment they had given him regarding Ursulo:

"I don't want to kill him," he said. "I won't kill him." And he lay his head on La Borrada's lap, closing his eyes tightly so he would not be able to see or hear and so he could lose himself in intense forgetfulness.

Today he was floating over all that was lost. Over the stubborn, conquering water. Over failed hopes and projects, broken spirits. Over vain effort and illusion, over what could have been but was not, like a piece of wood, like a boat adrift, a slow corpse.

His body had become jammed with branches and thick mud at the corner of the house. But he could no longer feel. His only attitude was his ignorance of everything. Everything, sky, water, and clouds. Death was ignorance.

He was ignorant of the fact that his wife had watched his murder, when the terrible priest stabbed him savagely in the throat. Those strange eyes had witnessed his death, but Adán could not now know that.

He did not know the details of what had happened. He had secured *La Cautibadora* after he had crossed the river with Ursulo and the priest. When he was bending over he felt the blow and then, almost instantaneously, a profound silence, that had lasted up to this moment.

He was ignorant of whatever happened after that silence began.

"What have you done?" Ursulo asked the priest.

The priest was unable to respond, and from that point on they did not exchange a single word.

Had he cried out? Who knows? The fact is that La Borrada thought: "They've just killed Adán." She tried in vain to find the body under the storm and deep of night. In vain. Everything in vain.

The first *zopilote* came down and lighted on Adán's body; it had a hideous neck and noisy wings, like those of a giant cockroach. It looked all around, at Cecilia, Calixto, Marcela, Ursulo, at those still alive, fearlessly staring at them, sizing them up with calculating coldness. "As soon as they die—it must be thinking—or as soon as they are unable to defend themselves . . . " Then, lowering its bald head, it began to observe that incredible body on which it was perched. It looked at it with a profound intelligence and would probably begin by devouring its eyes, which are hard, consistent, and like the absolute condensation of the forces of that body's being. The eyes, and then immediately following the general plunder, the banquet.

The others no longer had any strength left. Those four human beings still alive, children of women, examples of mankind, links in our immense, beloved, and noble human chain, could do nothing. They looked at the filthy and foul-smelling buzzard, lacking the will and intelligence to resist and fight.

The fierce bird was vacillating on top of the corpse, and had still not decided to bury its beak into the eyes. It was an intelligent, keen bird, able to discover rotting flesh in the very center of the earth.

"Just as long as it doesn't go for Chonita," Ursulo still managed to think right before he died.

Tzotl, garbage. *Pilotl*, act of picking up or collecting. Garbage, infinite garbage.

Everyone was waiting suspensefully for the spectacle of the banquet, thinking of when their turn would come. They were about to witness something unspeakable. To witness the most extraordinary obscenity.

As she contemplated this nightmare, Marcela recalled the undefined perhaps concave impression (as if a gust of strange, distilled air had suddenly entered her mouth) she had experienced many years earlier, while reading a news article in which a North American journalist was describing the execution of a criminal in the electric chair. It was a narration from another world: completely unreal, incredible, and simple.

The journalists arrived two hours early so they could be searched. The North American narrator's colleagues had offered him whiskey.

"Oh, no," Marcela remembered his answer, "I want to maintain my mental independence."

"That doesn't have anything to do with it, understand? It's just that afterward it's intolerable. There's an odor, how can I put it, an odor that you never forget. Take a good drink. Those who come here for the first time need it more than we do. I've seen more than thirty executions and they all wind up being boring, believe me. I could simply go home and write up my notes without having to be here to see it. But the thing is that I'm trying to convince myself of something: I can't quite define it but I can't really forget it either. I'm talking about the smell. It always seems to be the same, but I believe that each man who has been burned in the chair has his own smell, his own personal, original smell."

The group of spectators then entered the "death chamber," a small, sober, sparsely furnished room.

It was not that Marcela remembered the actual details of the article, but, rather, simply the impressions it produced in her, how the story had ignited and excited the unexpected jungle of her imagination. That "death chamber" was so similar to the church sacristy in the village! And the village? What would become of it now that it was in its death throes, the cursed victim of the avenging water? What was to become of the empty, now utterly hopeless soul? Why the efforts to stay alive? The walls of the sacristy were bare; there were not even statues. Several sturdy, absolutely desolate chairs scattered around the room, and then the opaque, timid light.

A priest entered the "death chamber" with the doomed man walking behind him. The "death chamber" could have been thought of as being black, perhaps dark. But Marcela insisted instead that it was gray, like the gray of the sacristy where in the highest and most important of the chairs a mysterious, invisible but real being, a kind of invisible Christ, was also being electrocuted every minute, his death redeeming secret guilts and ungodly sins. Nevertheless, what did Adán redeem? What did they, Ursulo, Calixto, Cecilia, and herself, Marcela, redeem? What did the North American criminal redeem? The criminal had a smile on his face. He sat down in the chair and they immediately put on the modest diver's helmet. In the chair. Later, perhaps, the condemned man's eyelids would tremble under the helmet, and then his entire body would shake with laughter, shake like a puppet on strings, vibrating between two poles, curiously between two, the positive and the negative, vibrating with laughter.

What Marcela in her own way was rethinking out in her memory was now expressed with literally the same words as those of the reporter.

"As a consolation we have the fact that science has established without room for doubt that death by electrocution is the least cruel death of all, and of course the quickest, the one *almost* not even felt by the victim. But right there before your eyes was the corpse of that man and with the corpse the terrifying idea that he *almost* did not feel the horrifying torture. A word as simple, mediocre, grammatically useless, and irritating as the word *almost* nevertheless signified the most unimaginable and barbarous nightmare."

Yes, all the spectators, journalists, officials, and even the priest himself raised their handkerchiefs to their faces so as not to breathe in the smell. They had all already had their drink of whiskey, even the priest. But I know that I have that same smell in me, and I should not cover my face. I know that I have all the misery and all the greatness of man inside of me. That I defecate and ejaculate and my entire body can become filled with pus. When I come to understand this I feel like crying, and I would cry like no one has cried in human history just to be able to smell the nauseating odor of my own flesh in flames or in the grip of electrical currents of a bestial murderous chair, because it is my odor, and the odor of the executed criminal was my own odor, the odor of a pig in flames and burning hair and grease.

The *zopilote* began to pick at Adán's face, causing the corpse to rock. The buzzard lost its balance, loudly flapping its wings, and flew up to perch on the rooftop. It was the victory of death. It took small hops, ever cautious, with some fear and awe, in the presence of what still remained there of life. They would die, nevertheless, they would all die, and the *zopilote* was a king, the king of creation.

The "death chamber," gray, with gloomy walls, and now suddenly colossal, was rising up all around them. Its walls covered the sky and existence itself.

A second *zopilote* descended, and then a third. Huddled together, they coldly and calculatingly sized up the situation as if nothing could possibly be hidden from them, not even thoughts, as if they were masters of destiny. They absolutely knew what Ursulo was thinking and they were simply waiting there for him to finish thinking it. And the same was true with respect to Marcela, Calixto, and Cecilia.

Ursulo was on his land, on his fifteen *hectares*. The soil had begun to deteriorate, but he had stubbornly insisted that everyone remain. "I am guilty of what is happening to us," it occurred to him.

This entire tragedy began right after the failure of the strike.

The black and cruel *zopilotes* ignored nothing, not even that. They were familiar with the whole of existence, corner by corner. The shipwreck victims were not going to die of hunger. First, blindness, two empty sockets instead of eyes, and then immediately following, the stomach, the iliac cavity, with its entire network of tissues.

Earlier, many years earlier, the group of shipwreck victims belonged to that superior class above *zopilotes* which is capable of defeating them.

Cecilia was a woman.

Marcela was a woman.

Calixto was a man.

Ursulo was a man.

"I can't have her now," Calixto said to himself, thinking about Cecilia.

Not today. Today they were nothing nor did they belong to any class.

The strike failed because the terrible exodus had taken place. No one wanted to stay on a dry land without rain beside a useless river and an unusable, cracked dam.

During the period of the exodus, from atop several beams, Ursulo was urging the migrating strikers to stay.

"What?" they said. "And eat dirt?"

Ursulo gathered all the strength from his soul and his life:

"Yes!" he shouted.

He climbed down from his rostrum and taking a fistful of earth from his fifteen *hectares* he thrust it into his mouth to swallow it.

"Why not?" he shouted again, sobbing.

The only ones to have understood that call were Jerónimo and Calixto.

The *zopilotes* knew all the secrets of the heart. Who had paid any attention to them before, when they would circle meekly and with quiet rhythm high in the skies so far away? Nevertheless, there always exists a bond of reciprocal vigilance and hatred between them and man.

The vultures are located at one extreme and man at the opposite. Man goes toward them and before he dies defends himself with the land or fire. The vultures wait. Their turn is written.

"I wonder," it occurred to Marcela, "if Jerónimo escaped the *zopilotes,*" and her deep affection for that beloved body was born in her once again.

Jerónimo had understanding, kind eyes that always looked full of tears. Jerónimo and Natividad had organized the union and then later the strike.

Natividad had anticipated everything that would happen.

"The water is no good," he explained. "Neither is the land. The Irrigation System could save itself, however, by introducing fertilizers, repairing the dam and establishing a large cooperative. If we lose the strike we lose everything."

They killed him.

Today, under the earth, he would also be saved from the *zopilotes*.

Cecilia was the earth, Ursulo's fifteen *hectares*.

The earth is a somber goddess. It has a cosmic origin, the nebula before condensation and fire, and it still exists. The earth demands the effort, dignity, and hope of man.

Natividad longed to transform the earth, and his doctrine supposed a new man who would be free on a new and free land. That is why Cecilia, who was the earth of Mexico, loved him, even though she did so unconsciously, even though she was ignorant of the secret, profound forces that determined such love.

Calixto and Ursulo represented something else. They were the bitter, blind, deaf, complex, contradictory transition toward something that waited for them in the future. They were the unformulated longing, the confused hope that rises up to ask what its road will be.

Chonita had died many, very many years before, the mysterious fruit of the desperate land. Today the *zopilotes* would devour her.

They seemed to meditate for an instant, but then, without the slightest hesitation, they flung themselves onto their victims.

Mexico City, December 1941–August 1942

José Revueltas (1914–1976), who is generally regarded as a central figure in Mexican literature, wrote novels, essays, criticism, short stories, film scripts, and plays. *Human Mourning* is his only full-length novel available in English translation.

Roberto Crespi is associate professor of Latin America literature at Oakes College, University of California, Santa Cruz. He received his Ph.D. in romance languages and literatures from Harvard University in 1972. Crespi has also translated *The Emigration Dialectic: Puerto Rico and the United States* by Manuel Maldonado-Denis (1976) and *Race and Class in Santo Domingo* by Hugo Tolentino Dipp (1978), and contributes to *Calibán, Latin American Perspectives, Crítica,* and *Casa de las Américas.*

Franklin Pierce College Library

00042253